"In *Finding Favor*, Brian Jones uncovers a treasure trove of God's favor for his people. Sometimes we wonder if God really wants to give us his favor—his supernatural intervention bringing blessing into our lives. But Brian makes sure we know that closed doors and sweeping floors—and a host of other things—are all in the realm of God's favor for us. Friends, do yourself a favor and read this book."

Kyle Idleman, author of *Not a Fan* and *Grace Is Greater*

"You've prayed for God's blessings. But what are you *really* asking for? How does God really bless us? In this eye-opening book, Brian Jones shares the answer in his engaging, straightforward, and incredibly practical style. It's a must-read for anyone wanting God's favor."

Vince Antonucci, pastor of Verve Church, author of *God for the Rest of Us*

"Do you want God's favor? I'm sure you do, because we all do. But none of us desires the struggle or pain that's experienced along the way. In *Finding Favor* Brian Jones helps us understand that God longs to give us his favor, but not before he makes us take a long hard look at ourselves."

Caleb Kaltenbach, author of *Messy Grace* and *God of Tomorrow*

"I'm old enough to be able to look back at a significant portion of my life and see the favor of God. One thing is obvious—it was not at all how I thought it would be. In *Finding Favor* Brian will help you to understand that the key word in the term 'favor of God' is 'God.' It's an excellent look at how God blesses us in ways that are best for us rather than just writing us a check. We all desire our Father's favor. Brian will help you understand it."

Tim Harlow, senior pastor, Parkview Christian Church, Orland Park, Illinois

"In thirty years of ministry, I've been enthralled by the glorious, unmerited favor of God that I've seen on display in the lives of countless saints. In those same thirty years, I've also been undone by the sorrows and sufferings of the beloved. Can the people of God face trouble in the world and still know themselves to be highly favored? Brian Jones's *Finding Favor* convincingly, winsomely cries yes! In Jones's inspirational new work, readers discover themselves highly favored in Christ whether on the mountaintop or in the valley."

Alan D. Wright, senior pastor, Reynolda Church, Winston-Salem, North Carolina, author of *Free Yourself, Be Yourself*

FINDING

GOD'S BLESSINGS
BEYOND HEALTH, WEALTH,
AND HAPPINESS

BRIAN JONES

IVP Books

An imprint of InterVarsity Press
Downers Grove, Illinois

InterVarsity Press
P.O. Box 1400, Downers Grove, IL 60515-1426
ivpress.com
email@ivpress.com

InterVarsity Press® is the book-publishing division of InterVarsity Christian Fellowship/USA®, a movement of students and faculty active on campus at hundreds of universities, colleges, and schools of nursing in the United States of America, and a member movement of the International Fellowship of Evangelical Students. For information about local and regional activities, visit intervarsity.org.

The material in chapter two that was first published in Pastors.com is used by permission.

While any stories in this book are true, some names and identifying information may have been changed to protect the privacy of individuals.

Published in association with the literary agent Don Gates of The Gates Group, www.the-gates-group.com.

Cover design: David Fassett
Interior design: Jeanna Wiggins
Images: padlock: © 35mmf2/iStock/Getty Images Plus
*   wooden door: © leskas/iStock/Getty Images Plus*

ISBN 978-0-8308-4523-1 (print)
ISBN 978-0-8308-8848-1 (digital)

Printed in the United States of America ∞

InterVarsity Press is committed to ecological stewardship and to the conservation of natural resources in all our operations. This book was printed using sustainably sourced paper.

Library of Congress Cataloging-in-Publication Data
A catalog record for this book is available from the Library of Congress.

P   25 24 23 22 21 20 19 18 17 16 15 14 13 12 11 10 9 8 7 6 5 4 3 2 1

Y   36 35 34 33 32 31 30 29 28 27 26 25 24 23 22 21 20 19 18

FOR DAD

CONTENTS

INTRODUCTION

IN THE EARLY MORNING HOURS of June 28, 2009, Honduran army special forces stormed Honduran president Manuel Zelaya's presidential palace under cover of night, disarmed his security detail, pulled him out of his bed, threw him into a plane, and dropped him on an airstrip in Costa Rica wearing his pajamas.

Within hours the capital city of Tegucigalpa erupted in chaos. Demonstrators against the coup put up roadblocks throughout the capital. The military responded by enacting martial law and forcing a total media blackout—shutting down TV stations, radio stations, and newspaper websites.

Then, off the plane walked yours truly in Bermuda shorts, a Hawaiian shirt, and sunglasses, completely unaware of what had transpired after we took off from Houston on a connecting flight from Philadelphia. My wife, Lisa, our three daughters, and I would be spending the week visiting missionaries our church was thinking about supporting financially. The coup happened while we were in the air. The airline didn't know about it, so we obviously didn't either; that was until we were greeted at the airport by armed soldiers and frightened families running in every direction.

Miraculously, I found Pablo, the local driver I had hired to take us each day to the different missionary outposts. Thank goodness he decided to stay and wait for us.

"What in the world is going on, Pablo?" I asked.

"Honduras had a coup," Pablo said with a thick Honduran accent. "Military in charge. Very dangerous. Airport shutdown. No flights in or out. Everyone told to stay home."

"What should we do?" I replied.

"Two options: you stay in airport, or we make run for it."

"Make a run for it?" I shot back.

"Yes. We don't have much time. Army says if anyone caught driving they throw them in prison. No questions."

I asked Lisa what she thought we should do. We looked at our three young girls, saw the declining situation in the airport, and quickly concluded that the best choice was to be with the missionaries four hours away in San Pedro Sula. There had been two prior coup d'états in Honduras in 1963 and 1975. Most Hondurans believe both coups had CIA fingerprints all over them. The way things were heading it would have been unsafe for anyone to stay in the airport very long, let alone a family of Americans. Whichever decision we made would be risky. (It turns out that Honduras at the time was the "murder capital of the world." The US State Department had issued a travel advisory—which I found out about *after* I returned—that stated more murders occurred in Honduras per capita than in any country on the planet. Americans were popular targets.)

"Okay, let's make a run for it," I said.

Within minutes we were loaded up and racing wildly through the streets of Tegucigalpa in the minivan of a total stranger I found on TripAdvisor two weeks prior.

I've traveled all over the world, and I have been in some tricky situations before, but I had never seen anything like this.

People were building large mounds of tires in the streets and lighting them on fire with gasoline to block traffic. Looters were sacking stores. Gangs in pickups sped past us with eight to ten men in the back holding rifles.

"Hey Dad, is everything okay?" I remember my youngest daughter asking.

"Everything's just fine," I told her. "We're going on an adventure. Pablo is going to be driving fast, so hold on."

Just outside the city we came upon a barricade of cars blocking the road, causing traffic to stop in both directions.

"Can we drive through it?"

"No!" Pablo said firmly.

We could see armed men ahead of us randomly pulling people out of their cars. Pablo rolled his window down as a man motioned for us to pull over.

"Military?" I leaned forward and asked.

"Don't think so," Pablo said as he shook his head side to side.

The man who waved us over asked to see our identification. The whole time I prayed that he didn't find out we were from the United States. Another man walked up beside him, pointed at us, and began peppering Pablo with questions. Pablo raised his voice as he waved his hands in the air, yelling at both of them. The only thing I could understand was the word *Americano*.

This is really bad, I thought.

More men with guns walked toward the van.

The man who stopped us began shouting back at Pablo, then, for some reason, walked around the van and opened the passenger side sliding door where I was sitting with the girls.

He stared at my three daughters for what seemed like an unconscionably long time.

I positioned my feet around the base of the seat, giving myself leverage in case I needed to lunge at him.

Then I prayed a quick prayer: "God protect us."

As soon as I mouthed the words his head snapped toward me. I stared back, both sets of eyes deadlocked. Then in what seemed like an instantaneous change in his demeanor, he smiled, nodded his head at me, turned back to Pablo, said something in Spanish, shut the door, yelled at the other men to back away, and then waved us on.

It was at that exact moment that I knew we were supposed to partner with the missionaries there to start new churches in Honduras.

Why?

What place needs the church more than the murder capital of the world where they overthrow their government as fast as teenagers post selfies on social media?

The coup, the scary people driving around in jeeps, and the dude carrying the rifle aimed at my family and me—they all lined up to confirm that this was the place we needed to go.

I didn't need to see anything else.

I was 100 percent convinced.

We were all-in.

In the seventh century, an Egyptian Christian monk named John Climacus was renowned for leading people to deeper levels of Christlikeness. In his book *The Ladder of Divine Ascent*, he outlined thirty virtues to be pursued that would lead one to grow closer to God (the thirty virtues were in memory of the thirty years of the life of Christ). "Fight to escape from your own cleverness," he advised. "If you do, then you will find salvation and uprightness through Jesus Christ our Lord."[1]

Climacus was saying that one of the greatest barriers to experiencing God's presence and power in our lives is our need to completely figure God out in advance of what he is doing, as a way of controlling him and predicting his next move. Yes, of course everything we believe must be rooted in Scripture, but like any great love story, God reveals more and more of himself to us the more we get to know him and his Word.

Years after our experience in Honduras I went through another series of strange circumstances that sent me to God's Word to understand what was happening.

This time a passage from the Bible leapt off the pages: "Surely, Lord, you bless the righteous; / you surround them with your favor as with a shield" (Psalm 5:12).

Something resonated deep inside of me that told me this was what I had been trying to understand.

Favor? I thought. *What is favor?*

I went to my Bible's concordance and looked up the word to see where else it occurred. To my shock it was *all over* the Bible.

How did I miss this? I asked myself, as I scoured passage after passage and story after story.

Here I was, a committed Christian for decades, a Bible-teaching pastor who went to seminary and had more than two decades' experience teaching the Bible, and the idea of God's favor was completely new to me.

The words of Augustine had never been truer than in my case: "The Bible was composed in such a way that as beginners mature, its meaning grows with them."[2]

I found a term for what I experienced in Honduras, as well as many times before and since: *God's favor.*

I had prayed for God's favor in one of the scariest moments of my life, and God responded by intervening and changing that man's mind from whatever he intended to do.

I believe God in his favor wants to do something in every area of your life. I'm not talking about good things or even great things, but *insanely* great things, not just in one area but in *every* facet of your life.

The question I have for you is, *Do you believe this?*

ONE

GOD'S FAVOR

It is doubtful whether God can bless a man
greatly until He has hurt him deeply.

A.W. TOZER, *THE ROOT OF THE RIGHTEOUS*

WHEN MY MIDDLE DAUGHTER was in seventh grade, she called home while away at an overnight Christian youth conference to tell us that she and her best friend were no longer going to date boys because they had decided to "date Jesus" instead.

I stopped her mid-sentence, put the phone to my chest, and laughed out loud.

"I'm serious, Dad. Why are you laughing?"

"Well for starters you're in seventh grade and haven't had a boyfriend yet. But mainly because that's the *silliest thing* I've ever heard."

"Well, that's what our conference speaker said we should do."

"That's because he's clueless."

"He is not clueless, Dad. He was being honest," she insisted.

"Well, dear, you're going to find out that in life, just because someone's a Christian and they're being honest doesn't always mean they have good judgment. Christians believe and say silly things all the time. Unfortunately, your workshop speaker is one of these types of Christians."

"Well, we've already texted the boys that like us and told them that we're only going to date Jesus from now on."

"Tell them that you were playing a prank, and while you're at it, text me the name of that speaker. He and I need to have a little chat."

"Why?"

"Because you *can't* date Jesus. What happens if two months into it you decide you don't like him? Are you going to break up with the Lord and Savior of the universe just to go to the eighth-grade prom with some kid named Jack?"

I could practically see her rolling her eyes at me through the phone.

Two minutes after we hung up from our conversation, she texted me the speaker's name and told me that she and her friend were both "back on the market" now. Usually, this isn't the type of news that a father of daughters likes to hear, but given the alternative in this circumstance, I was all right with the outcome.

You might be surprised to know "dating Jesus" doesn't even crack the Top 10 of the most "well-meaning but misguided pieces of advice I've heard one Christian give to another." Not by a long shot.

HOLY AMBITION?

If you're new to the Christian faith, there's something I probably ought to warn you about. You're going to find that the longer you follow Jesus, the more you're going to bump into well-intentioned but odd statements by Christians that keep getting tossed around, sort of like "urban legends of Christianity." These beliefs *sound* like they could have their basis in the Bible (which is why they keep getting shared), but they actually don't.

Here's the one my seventh-grade daughter was taught: *Parents should discourage teenagers from dating.*

While I agree that dating should be put off as long as possible, there's nothing in the Bible that teaches this. (The best advice I ever heard about how to handle boys who want to date my three daughters was from NBA basketball legend Charles Barkley: "Kill the first one and hope the word spreads." I'm pretty sure that's in the Old Testament somewhere.) Compounding the problem with this specific misstatement, many well-meaning youth pastors encourage their students to do things like "date Jesus" instead (e.g., "focus on your relationship with God instead of dating").

Here's another popular misstatement that many Christians believe: *Full-time Christian ministry is God's highest calling.*

This is the belief that if you really want God to do something great with your life, you have to become a full-time pastor or a missionary to do it, preferably in another country with really poor people. If you don't, then your job is to pray for the people willing to do this and give money to support their efforts. Of course, this isn't how it is stated, but it is certainly how it comes across.

Years ago I went with a group of twenty guys from our church to attend one of the largest gatherings of Christian men in our country's history. The conference was electrifying. The messages, so transparently delivered, combined with the gutsy conversations we had as a group afterward, made this one of the greatest spiritual moments of our lives. Except for one person.

Ray walked with his head to the ground as the other men shared how the last few days were a game changer for them spiritually. I made him stop and then asked him what was wrong.

"This was great for all the guys here, except me!" he said.

"What do you mean?" I asked.

"My job," he fired back. "I hate my job. I just can't stomach the thought of getting up tomorrow morning and going into that office. I've been working there for twenty years. Every time I walk in there, I feel the cement hardening around my feet."

"Well, what do you want to do with your life?" I asked.

"Build decks," he shot back without hesitation.

I laughed until I realized he was serious.

"Wait, I'm sorry. Build decks? Like decks outside people's homes?"

"Yes, I'd build decks. But I can't. With my wife, kids, and a mortgage, I need the money. I'm stuck."

I thought to myself, *He makes more money than five of these other guys combined. Any one of them would kill to walk into his corporate office tomorrow morning.*

I could hear the desperation in his voice, so I looked into his eyes and said, "Ray, when you're a follower of Jesus, you're *not* stuck. *Go build decks!* Do it for the glory of God and don't look back!"

What shocked me about Ray's reaction to the conference was that it never occurred to him that God might actually be concerned about his job. It never occurred to him that God might be just as concerned with his life *outside* of church services as what happens *in* them.

The problem was that for Ray ambition was bad. It was something to be avoided. It wasn't holy. The impression he got from the conference (and growing up in church) was that the desire to completely abandon himself to God's will and do something insanely great with his life was okay, as long as he wanted to serve God as a missionary in Haiti. But building decks? There's no chapter and verse in the Bible that describes that calling.

Chances are you might have been given this mistaken impression as well. Listen, let's acknowledge that *selfish* ambition is a bad thing (Philippians 2:3). But godly ambition—the desire to self-sacrificially be used by God to the fullest—is a beautiful thing to behold. There's a world of difference between godly ambition and selfish ambition. One is encouraged, the other is condemned.

More important, godly ambition doesn't mean that to do something great with your life you need to go to seminary.

God's vision has always been for his people to serve him wherever they are, from the ends of their driveways to the ends of the earth. Get rid of this idea that you have to "go over there" for God to do something great through you.

God does want to do something great with your life. But please understand that it honestly doesn't matter *what* you do, as long as you do it to the glory of God.

The great Christian philosopher Elton Trueblood wrote, "It is a noble thing to be a Christian pastor, nourishing the common life and curing sick souls, but it is no more a holy task than that of a Christian banker."[1] Trueblood meant that God wants us to view every area of our lives as holy ground. Your boardroom is holy ground. Your baby's nursery is holy ground. Your venture capital meeting is holy ground. It's *all* holy ground in the eyes of the Lord.

But part of doing holy work includes doing it the way it was meant to be done: with every ounce of our beings as an act of worship. Holy ambition honors a holy God. Half-hearted efforts at raising a teenager won't cut it. Neither will approaching retirement without a plan for how you'll use your most unrestricted years to serve God. "Whatever you do," the apostle Paul said, "work at it with all your heart, as working for the Lord" (Colossians 3:23). There's no ambiguity about what Paul meant. *Whatever* you do, give it *everything* you have to give.

In his book *Success to Significance*, Christian businessman Bob Buford said that when he dies he wants his family to put an inscription on his tombstone that reads, "100X."[2] He got the idea from a parable Jesus told about how the Christian life is like a farmer who instead of methodically planting seed in neat, tidy rows, just started winging it everywhere.

Some of it fell on the hood of his neighbor's minivan. Others fell on the sidewalk. Some blew into the eyes of an elderly couple walking on the sidewalk. (Okay, I *may* be taking some creative license in retelling the story, but Jesus' point was the farmer recklessly sowed seed all over the place.) But a few seeds, miraculously, fell on good soil, which represents people who are open to the message of Jesus and ready to be used by him. These people, Jesus said, "hear the word, accept it, and produce a crop—some thirty, some sixty, some a hundred times what was sown" (Mark 4:20).

Buford said he wants to be a 100X kind of Christian. *Do you?*

As a pastor, I've had countless conversations with men and women with a similar story—Christians hungry to be used by God who know that anything less than God-sized dreams for their lives is not enough. They've been told that God is "able to do immeasurably more than all we ask or imagine, according to his power that is at work within us" (Ephesians 3:20), and they want to experience that.

If you're the kind of person who wants to see a 100X return in every area of your life, I have very good news for you.

You don't have to be a pastor or missionary, though God can use those people.

You don't have to be a visionary person, though God can use that.

You don't have to be a natural leader, though God can certainly use that too.

You don't have to be attractive, a great speaker, a graduate of a prestigious college, come from a strong family, or have personal magnetism.

You only need one thing . . .

You need the favor of the Lord.

If God lays his hand on your life and gives you his favor, no army is too strong, no task too great, and no challenge too daunting for God to accomplish what he wants to accomplish through you.

THE FAVOR OF GOD

God's favor is his supernatural intervention to bring a blessing into your life.

Can you think of anything that would be more advantageous than seeking and finding the favor of the Lord to give you the supernatural assistance you need to solve your problems, be present in your trials, and make your hopes a reality? With your family? At your work? In your world?

Think of the lengths people in the marketplace go to in order to find a competitive advantage to grow their business. Consider all the apps, systems, tools, and tips we have at our disposal to help us become more organized. Reflect on what parents do to give their children every possible advantage in life. We're all looking for "the thing" that will help us become everything God created us to be in every area of our life. *God's favor is that thing.*

Moses discovered that with God's favor he could successfully lead a ragtag group of slaves to bring the most powerful army in the world to its knees. *Gideon* knew that with God's favor he could successfully discern which path God wanted him to take in his life. *Nehemiah* asked for God's favor and was granted the opportunity to successfully lead the most significant building project in the nation of Israel's history, despite severe opposition.

An important thing to understand, however, is that God's favor will not keep you from experiencing personal hardship. As much as I'd like to tell you that God's favor will make your life so easy that you'll be able to eat ice cream and go to bed and lose weight (let's admit that would be pretty awesome), it doesn't work like that. *Daniel* was shown God's favor, but spent the rest of his life in exile in Babylon. *Joseph* was shown God's favor, but had a terrible childhood and spent the majority of his adult life away from his family. *Esther* was shown God's favor, but almost got herself killed fulfilling God's call on her life.

Yet, despite the difficult journeys the great men and women in the Bible sometimes endured, they all understood there was *nothing* more important than seeking the favor of the Lord before anything they did. With it, victory was ensured. Without it, the battle was lost before it began.

What could God accomplish through your finances if you had his favor on them? What could happen in your quest to find the right person to marry if God's favor was on that quest? What could happen if you sought and found God's favor for that new business idea of yours?

Keep in mind, though, favor is not magic. We don't control God's favor any more than we control God himself. No amount of positive thinking, visualization, or manipulative self-help mind tricks will bring favor to pass. God's favor is his and his alone to disperse.

One more thing: God will withdraw his favor if we deliberately disobey his commands.

The Old Testament king Manasseh sinned greatly against the Lord, and he was led away into captivity by a neighboring army. "In his distress," we're told, "he sought the favor of the Lord his God and humbled himself greatly before the God of his ancestors" (2 Chronicles 33:12). The good news, for him, and for us is, "When he prayed to him, the Lord was moved by his entreaty and listened to his plea" and delivered him from their hands. Favor can be given, taken away, and then given again. It is God and God's alone to decide. Our task is simply to obey and to ask.

It's clear that there's nothing more important than having God lay his hand on your life and go with you to face your challenges as a man or woman, husband or wife, student, parent, police officer, or CEO. If maximum impact is your aim, then the favor of the Lord is what you must seek.

JACOB THE TRICKSTER

Thousands of years ago there was a man named Jacob. God had big plans for Jacob's life, just like he does for you and me.

"Your descendants," God told Jacob, "will be like the dust of the earth" (Genesis 28:14). That's a pretty incredible vision for someone's life, especially when you realize how impossible this sounded to Jacob at this point in his life. If Jacob's brother Esau had his way, both Jacob and his children wouldn't have lived to see another day.

Esau hated Jacob.

Jacob's tumultuous relationship with his brother began at birth, as fraternal twins. The first child came out of the womb with a head full of hair, so his parents gave him the name Esau, which in Hebrew meant "hairy." The second one came out just seconds behind, grasping the heel of his older brother. He was given the name Jacob, which in Hebrew meant "he grasps the heel." Figuratively, however, Jacob meant "he deceives."

If Jacob's parents were somehow to purchase the *5,000+ Best Hebrew Baby Boy Names* book, my guess is Jacob wouldn't have been one of the more popular choices. Nowadays you'll meet plenty of guys with this name, but for this Jacob, his name was a curse that would become a self-fulfilling prophecy.

Someone once said, "We are never more than six inches from our childhood." That's never been truer than with Jacob and Esau.

The circumstances of their birth would serve as a metaphor for the rest of their lives

Once when they were teenagers, Esau came back from spending one too many days hunting in the wilderness on the brink of starvation. Sensing an opportunity to take advantage of his brother's weak state of mind, Jacob tricked him into giving him his birthright in exchange for a bowl of soup (Genesis 25:31).

A Hebrew firstborn son's birthright meant that he would be given a double portion of his father's inheritance (Deuteronomy 21:17).

Cheating your brother out of his inheritance for a fifty-cent bowl of chili?

What a jerk.

But it gets worse.

Another time, when their father was near death, Jacob put animal skin on his arms and convinced his near-blind elderly father that he was Esau. And he stole the blessing that was meant for his brother (Genesis 27:22-29). This blessing was a powerful moment anticipated by Jewish young men when their fathers were on their deathbeds. They would be drawn close to hear their father's dreams for their future in intimate detail, and his wishes for how they were to conduct themselves after his passing. It was a poignant rite of passage that Jacob stole from Esau.

"Isn't he rightfully named Jacob?" his brother Esau screamed when he found out what had happened.

Esau knew there was only one thing left to do: *murder his brother.*

Jacob ran away from Esau to their uncle's family, hundreds of miles to the north. For the next twenty years Jacob lived in exile, and yet he also prospered—he got married, had twelve sons (who would later become the heads of the twelve tribes of Israel), and became a wealthy breeder of cattle. Everything was perfect in Jacob's *new* life, except for one thing: he wasn't actually home.

After two decades away, God tapped Jacob on the shoulder and told him it was time to go back home and make things right. Jacob decided to obey and headed out. After days of travel, Jacob and his family arrived at nightfall on the outskirts of his childhood homeland. One more day's journey and it would be the first time Jacob would have stood face to face with Esau since Jacob betrayed him.

Jacob sent his family on ahead while he slept on the bank of the Jabbok creek, alone.

Oswald Chambers wrote, "You may often see Jesus Christ wreck a life before He saves it."[3] That's exactly what happened that night with Jacob.

Genesis 32:24 tells us that an unknown man attacked him, and the two wrestled until daybreak. It was a cage match for the ages, a mix between WrestleMania, an MMA fight, and Rocky versus the Russian guy at the end of Rocky IV. Because of the cover of night, Jacob could not see who he was fighting.

The symbolism here is quite striking. When life isn't working as planned, how often have we wrestled through long, sleepless nights with an unknown assailant? Is it God we're frustrated with during these times of doubt? Is it Satan, our adversary, we cannot see? Is it ourselves we're fighting? Is it circumstances? Maybe it's all of the above.

Sensing that there was something to be gained from this dark night of the soul, Jacob held on to the man until Providence gave up what he came to that riverbank to get. "I will not let you go unless you bless me," Jacob told his adversary (Genesis 32:26).

Hundreds of years later the prophet Hosea retold this story for his audience and shared two important pieces of information missing from the original. First, the adversary Jacob was wrestling with was an angel. You believe in angels, right? If you don't, you should. There are nuttier things you could be accused of believing.

Second, we're told that Jacob "struggled with the angel and overcame him; he wept and begged for his favor" (Hosea 12:4).

"Favor" doesn't appear in the version of this story in Genesis. Hosea wanted to make sure we understood that Jacob didn't need a polite blessing from God, the kind people send your way when you sneeze. He needed an intervention.

I don't know about you, but I'm sick of reaching out for help with my life and being offered well-intentioned blessings by Christians, sort of repackaged self-help principles masquerading as biblical truth. "For what am I to myself without You," Augustine asked in the *Confessions*, "but a guide to my own downfall?"[4]

I don't need improvement. I need the hand of God to reach down to me in my distress and knock walls down, open up seas, and shut the mouths of lions. I need total renovation, not a fresh coat of paint. What you and I need is God's favor.

And that's exactly what Jacob received.

THE MAGNIFICENT DEFEAT

The problem was Jacob's blessing was not what he thought he needed.

At the very least Jacob wanted God to make sure his brother didn't whack him and his whole family, Tony Soprano style. A lukewarm reception would have been wonderful. Reconciliation? Unthinkable, but that would have been icing on the cake.

But that's not what happened, initially at least.

The angel pulled a supernatural jujitsu move on Jacob and permanently wounded his hip. How's that for favor?

On top of that, the angel forced Jacob to say his name out loud (presumably as a way of forcing him to acknowledge the appropriateness of his name as a fitting description of what he had become). "They shall say no more," the original Hebrew reads in Genesis 32:28. No longer will anyone call you the "deceiver," the angel said, for you have fought with God and walked away transformed. His new name would forevermore be Israel, which meant "he who struggles with God."

Arising at dawn from the fight, with a new name and a debilitating limp, Jacob looked at the ground on which his battle with God had taken place. He called it Peniel, which means "face of God."

"It is because I saw God face to face," Jacob said, "and yet my life was spared" (Genesis 32:30).

No doubt there are hospital rooms, walking trails, and driver-side seats of cars that you look back on as places of Peniel too.

I believe God has led us here, to *this* riverbank together, because you are on the verge of getting tangled up in an inescapable fight for God's favor, a holy collision between divine providence and human brokenness.

We both want the finest blessings God has to offer. We both want God to watch over us. We want our prayers answered, our family members' diseases healed, and our good friends' problems solved.

Yet some part of us has to know that we can't experience God's favor until we've fought with God for his blessing. Some part of us must know that while fighting into what the great playwright Eugene O'Neill called the "long day's journey into night," we will not walk away unscathed.

The fight *will* be fierce and the hours long.

We *will* acknowledge the darkest parts of ourselves in the process.

But come morning we will come away from our own Peniel experience with a new self-understanding and a new vision for how God is going to work in our lives.

I'm not sure what unanswered prayer has been frustrating you. Whether it's for your job, health, finances, or family.

All I know is that I've learned it's possible to be favored by God, to be blessed by him, immensely even, for God to answer our prayers miraculously and not even realize that it has happened.

Favor rarely gives us want we want, no matter how much we squint, make threats, or roll around in the mud, but it always gives us *exactly* what we need. So often we pray for God to instantaneously fix our problems. What happens, more often than not, is he blesses us by giving us a limp.

In the following chapters, we're going to look at eight unexpected ways God blesses people with his favor. A few will be familiar. Most will not, at least by TV evangelist standards. But all are examples of divine intervention and blessing nonetheless.

If you're willing to read these next eight chapters with an open mind and a searching heart, you just might find what you're looking for.

God's favor is rarely understandable or predictable.

But it is always exactly what we need.

TWO

INVOLUNTARY PERSEVERANCE

*We are all faced with a series of great opportunities
brilliantly disguised as impossible situations.*

CHUCK SWINDOLL, *MAN TO MAN*

W E'VE BEEN CONSIDERING the different ways God responds
when we ask him to place his favor on our lives. One way
he responds, to our dismay, seems rather stark: instead of opening
new doors to explore new opportunities he slams doors shut. He
says no to our request to move on.

No matter how mad or frustrated this makes us, God forces
us to stay where we are, at least for a season, so that he can
finish his work in our lives.

Sometimes God's favor means he calls us to step out and start a new venture, and sometimes it means he calls us to stay put.

This shocks many of us. Closed doors are the last thing we thought we would receive when we prayed for God's favor. "I thought I was going to be *blessed*," we say, not realizing that God limiting our options can be one of his greatest blessings of all.

The Bible talks a lot about perseverance—about choosing not to quit. The part nobody talks about is what happens when the choice is made for us, and God *won't let us* resign, end a relationship, close a business, or drop a class.

Sometimes God responds to our requests for new assignments by saying, "I don't care how much you say you hate it. I'm not going to let you quit. I can't do a great work *through* you until I do a great work *in* you. You're going to stay the course. This is the way I'm choosing to show you my favor right now."

Are you willing to accept this aspect of God's favor? Are you willing to submit your plans and dreams to a God who will double bolt all your escape routes at a moment's notice? This may not be what you assumed God's blessing would look like, but he does this for a reason.

No one accomplishes anything of note by going from one unfinished task or relationship to the next. We can't assume that because of pain, boredom, or the desire for a fresh start, somehow God will make an exception for us.

I wonder what doors you've been bumping into lately. Job offers that haven't come through? Marriage proposals that haven't materialized? Small business loans that haven't been approved? Friends that have yet to be found? Situations that need to change for your kids?

Do you realize how these locked doors might be signs of God's favor, not an absence of it?

I've struggled with this many times over the years.

In college, I did an internship at a church where some well-meaning person slipped the pastor a book that talked about how Korean Christians went to their church buildings at 5 a.m. every day to pray. That was all it took.

For thirteen weeks straight I was required to get up at 3:45 a.m., take a shower, get dressed, and then make the fifty-five-minute commute to the church building just in time to hit my knees and join the faithful.

For sixty minutes of prayer.

On my knees.

Every flipping morning.

For thirteen straight weeks.

I kid you not.

"The Koreans are doing it, and their churches are growing like wildfire," I remember him telling me.

"That's great," I said, "but can't God hear us just the same at 9 a.m.? And does it need to be a whole hour? My knees start killing me after twenty minutes. After thirty minutes I'm getting butt cramps. After forty-five, honestly, I'm contemplating converting to Zoroastrianism."

I tried everything within my power to get out of that internship. I complained. I made phone calls. I tried *everything*, but I couldn't leave. I needed the internship for graduation.

Finally, after weeks of smashing my face into one closed door after another, I shut up, accepted that this was God's will for this season of my life, and got back to work.[1]

To my surprise, I look back on that summer internship as one of the most amazing learning experiences of my life. That pastor has become my mentor, and I find myself using things I learned that summer at the church I now serve—even waking up at 5 a.m. every day to pray in my home office . . . sometimes.

Has this ever happened to you? Have you ever tried getting out of something but couldn't, then later realized that maybe God was keeping you in that situation for your benefit? That maybe the lack of his response to your prayer was a response and was actually a sign of his favor?

What's encouraging is that all of us, including the giants of our faith, have or will face this dilemma.

WHAT IS IT?

Too bad Moses lived long before the seventeenth-century writer François Fénelon and didn't hear his advice: "Give yourself up to His plans. Be led wherever He wills by His providence."[2]

I think he would have appreciated the counsel.

God raised up Moses to stand up to the pharaoh of Egypt and lead God's people out of four hundred years of bondage and take them to the land God had promised them. God, through Moses, gave Pharaoh the option to let the Israelites leave peacefully. He refused, so God sent one plague after another—frogs, fleas, boils, locusts, country music, nonstop reruns of the TV sitcom *Full House*—just terrible, terrible things.

Finally, Pharaoh let them go, but changed his mind and cornered them at the Red Sea. God intervened, parted the water, led them across on dry land, drowned Pharaoh's army, and then led the Israelites to Mt. Sinai to receive the Ten Commandments. As a newly freed people, under God's law, led by Moses, they headed to the Promised Land in Palestine.

Unfortunately, on reaching their destination, they gathered intel that told them the people living there were frightening. Fearful of dying, they chose not to enter the land, and as a result were cursed by God to wander in the desert until the entire generation of people who didn't have faith to enter the land died.

It's at this point, in Numbers 11, we find Moses dealing with what had to be the most unenviable leadership job ever: *overseeing one million complainers.*

Numbers 11:4-6 tells us,

> The rabble with them began to crave other food, and again the Israelites started wailing and said, "If only we had meat to eat! We remember the fish we ate in Egypt at no cost—also the cucumbers, melons, leeks, onions and garlic. But now we have lost our appetite; we never see anything but this manna!"

"The rabble," arguably the second best nickname ever for a group of people, right after the team name "Clown Punchers" (from the movie *Dodgeball*), was a group of people who had joined God's people along their travels. They weren't Israelites but people who had come along for the ride. These people started complaining about the lack of meat in the desert, which in turn affected the attitudes of the Israelites, who should have known better.

Manna was a substance that miraculously appeared every evening to feed God's people in the desert. It was no doubt the backdrop behind Jesus' teaching to pray for "our daily bread" (Matthew 6:11). We're told that they'd gather it, crush it, and bake it into cakes. *Manna* means "What is it?" which, you have to admit, is pretty funny.

"What is that you're eating?" someone would ask.

"What is it?"

"No, *I* asked what is it."

I said, "What is it?"

"Ugh."

No doubt the humor behind the name wore off after eating it every single day for years.

Their constant complaining made Moses so angry that he lashed out at God for putting him in the unenviable position of serving as their leader:

> Why have you brought this trouble on your servant? What have I done to displease you that you put the burden of all these people on me? Did I conceive all these people? Did I give them birth? Why do you tell me to carry them in my arms, as a nurse carries an infant, to the land you promised on oath to their ancestors? Where can I get meat for all these people? They keep wailing to me, "Give us meat to eat!" (Numbers 11:11-13)

The pressure was too much, which is surprising when you look at everything Moses had been through. It wasn't the life and death showdown of facing the world's most powerful ruler that made Moses want to quit. It was listening to God's people complain every day. Faced with the never-ending prospect of being unable to satisfy all their demands, Moses asks for the unthinkable:

> I cannot carry all these people by myself; the burden is too heavy for me. If this is how you are going to treat me, please go ahead and kill me—if I have found favor in your eyes—and do not let me face my own ruin. (Numbers 11:14-15)

Notice that it wasn't the threats of Pharaoh's army that caused Moses' desperation. It wasn't the chariot wheels clacking in the distance as their archers pulled their bows. It wasn't the view of the raging ocean on one side, the army on the other, and certain death in the middle. It was the people—complaining in their tents, snickering as Moses walked by. He could see the contempt in their eyes. Their words were a constant dripping in the background of his daily routine.

That was enough to make him wish he were dead.

HUMILITY THROUGH PERSEVERANCE

Once when the poet David Whyte had a chance to speak to the Benedictine monk Brother David Steindl-Rast, he asked him for advice about the next steps he should take in his career. While talking about the weariness he was feeling at the time, he told Brother David, "Speak to me about exhaustion." His response: "You know the antidote to exhaustion is not necessarily rest. The antidote to exhaustion is *whole-heartedness*. The reason you're so exhausted is that much of what you are doing you have no affection for."[3]

So many people try to make themselves feel better with vacations and time off when what ails them deep down is the direction their feet are pointed, not the pressures they're facing. If the intensity of your workload isn't the problem, more rest won't be the solution.

Isn't it amazing what we can endure when we love what we're doing? Here Moses was, facing more stress from Pharaoh than any one human being should have to face in a lifetime, yet it never debilitated him. The more Pharaoh gave, the more Moses gave right back. The leadership challenge made Moses come alive inside. But the moment Moses had to face something he didn't have affection for, he wilted.

Here's what I find interesting: God didn't let Moses quit, no matter how much he hated what he was doing.

"If I have found favor in your eyes," he told God, "do not let me face my own ruin." God knew he wasn't going to die being forced to listen to a bunch of whiners any more than he'd face his ruin in the shadow of the pyramids.

But Moses didn't understand that God did show him favor, and it was by *not* fulfilling his request. He helped lighten his load by recruiting seventy leaders to come by Moses' side to help (Numbers 11:24), but he didn't allow him to quit. Why?

The next chapter says, "Now Moses was a very humble man, more humble than anyone else on the face of the earth" (Numbers 12:3). I find this verse humorous for a couple of reasons.

First, how exactly does one know they are the humblest person on earth? Was there an annual humility Olympics historians don't know about?

Second, *many Bible scholars believe Moses wrote the book of Numbers!* Think about that for a moment. The humblest person in the world tells us he is, well, the humblest person in the world. (Other scholars believe a later editor inserted the comment. Sounds convincing to me.)

The point the book of Numbers makes is that God had a plan for Moses, quite possibly to do everything that was written in the book of Joshua—to lead them into the Promised Land and govern them afterwards. (The events in Numbers 11–12 occurred *before* God told Moses that he wouldn't be the one to lead the Israelites home.) This miraculous feat would require a staggering amount of humility to pull off, which, as anyone knows, comes not from being successful but from being humbled. Doing something one no longer has affection for, for a long period of time with no possibility of escaping it, has a way of eviscerating one of all matters of pride.

"The Lord cannot fully bless a man until He has first conquered him," A.W. Tozer wrote. "The degree of blessing enjoyed by any man will correspond exactly with the completeness of God's victory over him."[4]

Moses was a conquered man, and if the frustrations he faced in the desert are any indication, he was a very blessed man indeed.

CONFESSIONS OF THE CONQUERED

Years ago, before moving to Philadelphia to start Christ's Church of the Valley, I planted another church in Dayton, Ohio. This church took off like a rocket and soared from 150 to 153 in four years. I mean it just zoomed at breakneck speed. After just a year, we got kicked out of the middle school where we were meeting and had to quickly renovate an old paint store to meet in.

Now, just so you understand, when I felt called to ministry, I began laying plans to start the single largest, fastest growing church in the history of human civilization. I was going to give credit to God, of course, but kind of like the actors who pretend to be *thoroughly surprised* when they win an Oscar and then pull out three pages of prepared notes when they get up to the podium.

I don't know what happened, but God didn't understand what I was trying to accomplish for me . . . I mean him. The church didn't grow. We attracted our own "rabble," a small group of people with the spiritual gift of complaining, just like the ones in Moses' congregation. Nothing I tried worked. I became depressed. Two years into this new church, I began praying for God to release me from this assignment.

The funny thing is once I started praying I started getting job offers. One was to plant a new church in West Palm Beach, Florida, with an effort funded by a billionaire celebrity CEO. (I'd tell you his name but that would be bragging. I'm not above bragging, but I am above getting sued, which I've been told could happen if I mention his name.) I was told he was friends with other celebrities who would join our new church. I was told that he thought I'd be perfect for the job, that I would make three times what I was making, and could use his yacht on the weekends.

I got a call from another organization that was planting a new church outside of Boulder, Colorado, arguably the prettiest city I've ever visited. The mountains we're stunning. The air was crisp. The field was ripe. The job was mine if I wanted it.

What happened with the job in Colorado? I blew the final interview. I mean I became argumentative over some obscure doctrine and melted down in front of everyone. It was embarrassing. My friends in the room were like, "What happened?" My wife said on the plane ride home, "What was that all about?" Looking back, I'm convinced I self-sabotaged the last twenty minutes of the interview. Deep down I knew I wasn't supposed to leave the church in Dayton.

The job in West Palm? I came to my senses halfway through the interview and told them that I couldn't be bought and that they'd better look elsewhere.

I flew home from the Colorado interview and walked through the doors of the ugly, dilapidated paint store we could afford to only partially renovate.

I sat down in my makeshift office/electrical closet/storage closest/entryway to the restroom area, buried my face in my hands, and said, "You're not going to let me quit, are you?"

The hum of the fluorescent light bulbs hung in the air as I sat in the emptiness of the moment.

"I have nothing left," I prayed.

Silence.

"I don't want to be here. You do understand that there's no part of me that wants to stay at this church, right?"

Silence.

"I mean the people hate me. Nobody thinks I'm very good at this. I've already proved that when it comes to"—then I cut myself off mid-sentence.

I couldn't stand to listen to the self-indulgent pity of my own voice any longer.

Oswald Chambers wrote, "When God gets us alone through suffering, heartbreak, temptation, disappointment, sickness, or by thwarted desires, a broken friendship, or a new friendship—when He gets us absolutely alone, and we are totally speechless, unable to ask even one question, then He begins to teach us."[5]

I don't know how you're stuck right now, or where you're stuck, or what you'd like to get out of but can't, but I want you to know that God taught me more about myself, about true character, about loving people, and relying on him over the next three years in that church than all of my years in ministry combined.

Not coincidentally, just when I had grown content with the idea of spending the rest of my life at that church, serving the wonderful people I had grown to deeply love, God called us to move to the suburbs of Philadelphia.

God's favor is funny like that.

Sometimes the most insanely great thing God will ever do in our lives will be the change he makes in us, not what he accomplishes through us.

THREE

HOLY DISCONTENT

*Modern man is drinking and drugging himself
out of awareness, or he spends his time shopping,
which is the same thing.*

<small>ERNEST BECKER, *THE DENIAL OF DEATH*</small>

HERE'S A RECENT SATURDAY MORNING text message conversation between the worship pastor on my church staff and me:

ME: "Been outside yet? Stunning. 15 people in church tomorrow."

WORSHIP PASTOR: "6 of them will be staff. ☺"

ME: "Can you blame them? It's gorgeous!"

In the suburbs of Philadelphia, there's a day each spring that clearly marks the end of winter. You know it when you see it—kids riding bikes, a warm breeze on your face, and people cutting grass for the first time.

As a pastor, whenever *that* day hits, I know that upcoming Sunday a sizeable number of our people will be worshiping at "Bedside Baptist" or skip church altogether to be outside.

This also marks the day many of our new Christians will take their first bite of the lotus plant.

THE LOTUS EATERS

In the ancient Greek playwright's epic poem *The Odyssey*, Homer tells the tale of the Greek military hero Odysseus's return home after the decade-long Trojan War.

Blown wildly off course, Odysseus and his fellow warriors spend years sailing from one island to the next, facing one obstacle after another, all in their quest to make it home to see their wives and children.

One of the early stops on their journey home was to the island of the lotus eaters.

When Odysseus and his men dropped anchor on the island to resupply, they were completely unaware that the island was a trap. Anyone who landed and ate the fruit of the lotus plant, which covered the island, never wanted to leave. The toxin of the lotus plant lulled them into sitting in the sun and relaxing, forever.

Sort of like the people in my area when the first day of spring hits.

Odysseus sent scouts to explore the island and find supplies, but they never returned. Then he sent more scouts to scout

out the scouts, but they didn't come back either. Finally, Odysseus personally went out with more scouts to scout out the scouts who had been scouting in the first place.

What he discovered astonished him: his fellow soldiers were sitting with their feet propped up, lazing about in the sun. None of them wanted to leave this tranquil place.

Homer writes, "Any crewmen who ate the lotus, the honey-sweet fruit, lost all desire to send a message back, much less return, their only wish to linger there with the Lotus-eaters, grazing on lotus, all memory of the journey home dissolved forever."[1]

Lost all desire? All memory of the journey home to their families dissolved forever? Had they never seen those emotional videos on YouTube of men and women in the armed forces surprising their spouses and kids when they return home from battle? (I cry every time I watch one of these videos. Not polite "please hand me a tissue" kind of tears either. I'm talking snot-dripping-down-my-shirt, "oh my gosh, this is so beautiful" kind of crying.)

How could it be possible that "all memory of the journey home dissolved forever"? These men had spent *ten years* away from their wives, families, and homeland!

Homer tells us that Odysseus knew he had to act fast or he'd lose his men for good. Recounting firsthand the drastic measures it took to recover his men, Odysseus says,

> I brought them back, back to the hollow ships, and streaming tears—I forced them, hauled them under the rowing benches, lashed them fast and shouted out commands to my other, steady comrades: "Quick, no time to lose, embark

in the racing ships!"—so none could eat the lotus, forget the voyage home.[2]

I want to make sure you can picture this last scene: battle-hardened warriors forcibly strapped to the bottom of the ship to keep them from diving overboard and swimming back to the island so they could sit in the sun all day.

That's the power of the lotus plant. Once you fall under its hypnotic spell, you can't free yourself from its power.

All help must come from the outside.

GET UP OUTTA THAT FUNK

What has always seemed strange to me about the Christian life is how often we find ourselves in situations we know we need to change but don't because in the words of Homer, we've "lost all desire."

We've grown content. But not content in the sense that we've assessed where we are and decided that we're not going to change because we're going to focus on other priorities.

I mean we've simply stopped caring. We've resigned ourselves to the fact that this is the mess we find ourselves in and can't muster the motivation to find a way out.

I'm not describing depression, though depression will sometimes mask the condition at hand. I'm talking about spiritual lethargy.

I'm talking about an unhealthy acceptance of a situation, relationship, or mindset that we know (and God knows) needs to change, but we simply won't.

Like staying in a job we hate.

Or putting up with an abusive relationship.

Or not seeking help when our kid has behavior issues.

Or continuing to coddle some addiction years in the making.

Or refusing to take care of our bodies.

Or not taking the steps necessary to take back control of our stressed out lifestyle.

Or remaining stuck in debt.

One bite of the lotus plant leads to another, and then another, until we grow content with being stuck.

Take, for instance, skipping church for *just* one day. It's not the one day that worries me. It's the one day that makes it a little bit easier to miss the next one and justify the one after that, and the month after that. Pretty soon you look back on an entire season of life when you haven't been engaged as a Christ-follower in the one thing we all know has the power to keep us focused and energized in our faith.

Such is the power of one bite of the lotus plant.

You walk into work one day and feel a nudge inside that today's the day to start looking for a new job. But doing so would be hard. And costly. And possibly require you to take a cut in pay.

So you don't.

You ignore that voice speaking deep inside of you and go out to lunch that day and order a steaming hot plate of lotus plant. It's delicious. It costs you nothing. There's no work required. You decide your job isn't that bad after all. You grow content. The dream of another venture fades.

Two weeks go by, and the desire weakens even more.

The following week you go out to eat *every day* at the lotus plant buffet, and before you know it two years have gone by, and the desire to change jobs has all but disappeared.

How is it possible that the same power that raised Jesus from the dead literally resides within us (Ephesians 1:18-20), and yet we can't lift our heads off the pillow sixty minutes early to create a new résumé?

Or go to the gym?

Or to couple's therapy?

Or cut up our credit cards?

Or go back to school to finish our degree?

Ancient Christian monks coined a term to describe the spiritual effects of the lotus plant. They called spiritual sloth and lethargy *acedia* (pronounced uh-see-dee-ah). It is a word formed by combining the Greek vowel *a,* which meant "no," with the Greek word *kedos,* which meant "to care."

Acedia means *I don't care anymore.*

Author Kathleen Norris wrote, "Acedia is like morphine. You know the pain is there, yet can't rouse yourself to give a d—."[3]

Herein lies the beauty of the various ways God answers our requests for his favor.

Sometimes, as I mentioned in chapter two, when we pray for God's favor, he responds by forcing us to stay where we are. Perseverance, it turns out, is often a character trait thrust upon us.

Other times, God in his infinite mercy makes us unable to live with ourselves any longer. He supernaturally reaches out and places a tiny spark of provocation in our hearts that over time erupts into a wildfire of holy discontent.

In response to our prayer, God shakes us out of our blind contentment, replacing our well-trod excuses with sacred rage—at our self-loathing and at lost time.

Acedia is indeed like morphine, so when we look at our comrades throwing off their shackles and jumping over the sides of our ships to swim back, we realize how fortunate we really are to be heading out to open waters.

Such was the case with Nehemiah the cupbearer.

BORN FOR THIS?

Nehemiah had one of those kinds of jobs that once you get them, you hold on to them for life.

Sort of like the guy I met who had a sweet gig lifeguarding on the beaches of Maui in the winter and leading fly-fishing trips on the Snake River in the majestic Grand Tetons in the summer. Or the professional chocolate taster I met who works at the Hershey Chocolate factory. Or professional mattress jumpers. Yes, there are people who get paid to spend the day jumping on mattresses for a living. *Best. Job. Ever.*

Nehemiah was the cupbearer to the king of Persia. The cupbearer was the guy who spent his days taking a sip of the king's wine before he drank it to make sure it wasn't poisoned. Possible death, every day, was a downside for sure, but this was outweighed by all of the other incredible perks of the job.

What were the perks? For one, because of his around-the-clock access to the king, Nehemiah, like other cupbearers before him (Tobit 1:22), was considered a close confidant to the Persian royal family. They trusted his counsel. On top of that, Nehemiah got all of his bills paid, and lived rent free in the royal palace. Then to sweeten the deal Nehemiah got to live in one of the coolest cities in the ancient world—the majestic ancient city of Susa.

But it wasn't just the perks that made Nehemiah want to hold on to his job. Like many people we know who've made steep sacrifices to get ahead in their careers, Nehemiah paid a high price to become a cupbearer. What was that?

Some scholars believe that Nehemiah had to become a eunuch.

You know what a eunuch is, right?

Kings wouldn't let men around their harems unless they were incapable of fooling around, so to land the job Nehemiah had to, um, make some sacrifices.

I can see the final interview now.

"So, Nehemiah, your references all checked out. One last question: How much do you want this job?"

Ouch.

And you thought going back to college to finish up your degree was rough?

Needless to say, Nehemiah was in no hurry to give up his job. He paid a big price to land the gig, and the perks were over the top.

Then, as luck would have it, Nehemiah writes,

Hanani, one of my brothers, came from Judah with some other men, and I questioned them about the Jewish remnant that had survived the exile, and also about Jerusalem.

They said to me, "Those who survived the exile and are back in the province are in great trouble and disgrace. The wall of Jerusalem is broken down, and its gates have been burned with fire." (Nehemiah 1:2-3)

Reality always has a way of ruining a perfectly good situation, doesn't it?

While Nehemiah was enjoying the perks of royal living, his fellow Jewish countrymen and women weren't faring so well. Back in his homeland of Israel, waves of Jewish leaders who had left Persia thirteen years earlier to rebuild the temple were going through terribly difficult times.

Decades before this happened, Nehemiah's great grandparents and many of God's people were carted off to where they now lived in exile. Many of God's people wanted to return home and rebuild their temple, the symbol of their country, but as often happens with pioneers, things went awry.

"When I heard these things, I sat down and wept," Nehemiah said (Nehemiah 1:4).

The whole book of Nehemiah tells the gripping story of how Nehemiah used his access to the king to gain permission to return to Israel with people and supplies to bolster the work of those serving back home.

In just fifty-two days Nehemiah rebuilt the walls that surrounded Jerusalem, providing much-needed protection from its enemies. Nehemiah supported the spiritual leader Ezra in leading the people to recommit themselves to God and his Word. He also reorganized and repopulated the city with other political and spiritual leaders. His work was fearless and extraordinary.

You could say that Nehemiah was born for this.

Which raises a simple question: Why did Nehemiah wait thirteen years to do this?

Why didn't Nehemiah leave with Ezra and his band of pioneers thirteen years prior (Ezra 7:7-8)? Why did he wait thirteen long years to engage in something he was born to do?[4]

Could he have been too young? Scholars agree that Nehemiah and Ezra were contemporaries, so it probably wasn't age.

Perhaps he didn't know how bad things were in Israel. But this is unlikely too, since we're told Nehemiah's brother Hanani brought back news of the settlers' desperate conditions. As someone with family on the ground, Nehemiah would have been especially interested in the status of the work there, and because he was so close to the king, he would have been able to receive near real-time updates about their progress.

Another possibility is that Nehemiah was considered a slave and was serving the king by force. We're not told that in the Bible, but it is a possibility. But if that were the case, he still could have asked to leave, just like he eventually did and was permitted to be sent out with people and resources. Why wait?

Why does someone wait thirteen long years to do something they were born to do?

We're not given a reason, but I'm pretty sure we can guess.

It's the same thing that holds us back when we know there's something we need to do but don't: *the lotus plant.*

Call it acedia, apathy, spiritual lethargy, or blind contentedness —it doesn't matter.

Nehemiah was stuck.

While we aren't certain that acedia was the cause, we do know that for thirteen years Nehemiah had a front-row seat to news flashes from the front lines, and did absolutely nothing about it. Why else would he wait?

The only thing we know for certain that Nehemiah did is he began praying for God's favor at some point during that thirteen-year stint. We know that because we see these references sprinkled throughout the book of Nehemiah:

~ "Lord, let your ear be attentive to the prayer of this your servant and to the prayer of your servants who delight in revering your name. Give your servant success today by *granting him favor* in the presence of this man." (Nehemiah 1:11)

~ "*Remember me with favor, my God*, for all I have done for these people." (Nehemiah 5:19)

~ "I also made provision for contributions of wood at designated times, and for the first fruits. *Remember me with favor, my God*." (Nehemiah 13:31)

My hunch is that at some point during the thirteen-year stretch that Ezra and the other pioneers were back in Israel, Nehemiah began praying for God's favor, and God answered that prayer by sending his brother Hanani.

We often don't know what we're going to get when we pray for God's favor, but as the poet Elizabeth Barrett Browning observed,

God answers sharp and sudden on some prayers,
  And thrusts the thing we have prayed for in our face,
  A gauntlet with a gift in't.[5]

Hanani showing up at the palace was no accident. For thirteen years Nehemiah remained numb. To his people's plight, to the role he could play, to his mission in life, to his life's work.

We can't fault him, we've been there, and more than likely we'll go there again at some point in the future. As the fourteenth-century German mystic Meister Eckhart observed, "We rarely find people who achieve great things without first going astray."[6]

But at some point Nehemiah prayed for favor, and God listened, just like he'll listen to you.

SOMETIMES THINGS HAPPEN

It's interesting how some objects appear innocuous by themselves, until we place them in the hand of someone we know.

Take laxatives, for instances. They're a useful form of medicine when taken appropriately. But I'll never forget the first youth outing I went on as a college intern. At the end of the night a convulsing fourteen-year-old girl handed me a half-consumed pack in tears.

"I'm bulimic. I don't know how to stop," she told me.

Or a twenty-dollar bill. We all use them. They're necessary. But I can't erase the memory of a fifty-five-year-old Christian woman I know buying a bottle of vodka with one. When our eyes met I could feel the weight of her addiction.

Or a smart phone. They're an essential part of our everyday life. We can't imagine not having one. But I can't tell you how many friends I have that can't stop looking at porn on them.

This will be the last time, they all tell themselves.

According to Amazon.com, one of the most highlighted passages of any book since the inception of their reading device, the Kindle—highlighted almost twice as often as any other passage—is from the second volume of *The Hunger Games*:

"Because sometimes things happen to people and they're not equipped to deal with them."[7]

None of us received training on how to answer acedia when it comes knocking on our door. Yet it comes, daily almost, peddling what Søren Kierkegaard called "the sickness unto death"—despair, and all of its damnable friends.[8] It comes with a smile, selling a tonic of relaxation and rest, but ends up delivering only evisceration trailed by a deadened soul.

A fourth-century monk, Evagrius Ponticus, talked a lot about acedia. He made a keen observation that I think would be wise to share with you now: "The further the soul advances, the greater are the adversaries against which it must contend."[9]

In other words, the more you grow in Christ, the forces that wage war against your soul will progressively become stronger and more cunning.

This should frighten us.

Evagrius Ponticus was right—we eventually get to the point where our enemy stops using full frontal assaults, and instead begins orchestrating a master strategy of deception built on tiny compromises.

"Let's just skip today because it's lovely outside. Besides, it's just one day."

"It's just one cheat meal. Just one extra hour of work."

"Just one day going to bed without resolving what to do with our kid's behavioral problems."

"Just one small charge on the credit card."

For two decades of my adult life I allowed myself to remain obese. If you asked people if I was overweight, they would have probably been nice and described me as a bit pudgy.

The fact is I was obese. At my highest, I weighed 272 pounds. I'm 6'2". That's a body mass index (BMI) of 34.9, which is not good.

I share this because it's easy to look at Nehemiah and shake our heads at how seemingly simple it was for him to allow thirteen years of his life to slip away. Missed opportunities. Lost conversations. More than a decade of staying on the sidelines of his life's work.

Nehemiah lost thirteen years of his life. I lost twenty.

How did it start? Just one tiny bite of the lotus plant. For 7,300 straight days, I put personal health out of my mind.

Then a few years back I did something radical.

I didn't go to Weight Watchers. I didn't start an Atkins quick-fix diet. And I didn't order workout videos to use at home. (Actually, I *did* order some workout videos, but I tried them for sixty seconds and said, "Lord take me home now. I'm *not* going to dance this weight off." Trust me; I looked ridiculous.)

I began praying for God's favor on my life. That's it.

Here's the kicker: I didn't pray for God's favor *so that I could lose weight*. I wasn't that specific. I mean, *I wasn't even thinking* about weight loss at the time. It was the farthest thing from my mind. I just wanted God to bless me any way he chose to do it. Praying for God's favor is a dangerous thing to do. You never know what you're going to get.

Then one day I was on my computer, and I looked at myself in a photograph of my family hiking.

I saw myself.

I mean we always *see* always ourselves in the mirror, but at that moment *I saw myself the way I actually was.* I saw myself as God saw me: loved, handsome, valuable, and unhealthy.

I looked at that photo and said, "*That's it.*"

At that moment God supernaturally intervened in my life and gave me a gift: *anger.* Anger at lost time. Anger at my hollow excuses. Anger at what could have been.

The great German theologian Jürgen Moltmann wrote,

Faith, wherever it develops into hope, causes not rest but unrest, not patience but impatience. It does not calm the unquiet heart, but is itself this unquiet heart in man. Those who hope in Christ can no longer put up with reality as it is, but begin to suffer under it, to contradict it. Peace with God means conflict with the world, for the goad of the promised future stabs inexorably into the flesh of every unfulfilled present.[10]

No one ever told me that hope in its purest form is often expressed through rage. I shouldn't have been surprised. Oppression is rarely overthrown politely.

Since I wanted to make a lifestyle change, I made the commitment to transform my body over an entire year's time. I made one year's worth of appointments with a dietician, and I hired a trainer to work with me two days a week.

I worked my tail off six days a week. I became fanatical about what I ate, how I prepared my food, and whether or not it was nutrient dense. It wasn't easy, but after seven months I hit my goal weight, having lost fifty-seven pounds while gaining significant muscle mass.

People asked how I did it. My answer: "I became angry enough to change." As Moltmann said, "Those who hope in Christ *can no longer put up with reality as it is.*"

How did I become angry enough to change after twenty years of living knee deep in the status quo? The only answer I can give is God's favor.

When it comes to acedia, help only comes from the outside.

I share this with you because I want you to know that whatever soul-numbing thing has you in its grasp, you can be free.

You don't have to stay on the island.

You *can* leave.

FOUR

INTENTIONAL
OBSCURITY

Ob·scu·ri·ty—noun

1. The state of being unknown or forgotten

2. Something that is difficult to understand

THE AMERICAN HERITAGE DICTIONARY

YEARS AGO I ASKED A RETIRED PASTOR how long it took him to write his sermons each week.

Bill was the kind of man the world too easily dismisses—no formal education and a tiny congregation—yet out of his mouth came an incredibly profound observation about preaching, and life.

"Some sermons take twenty minutes to write. Others take a lifetime."

When Vincent van Gogh walked to the pulpit in October 1876 to preach his very first sermon, we're not told how much time he spent in study beforehand.

All we know is that van Gogh had big shoes to fill. His father and grandfather were both preachers of note. As he gripped the lectern, the weight of their expectations surely pressed on him. "It is an old faith . . . that our life is a pilgrim's progress—that we are strangers in the earth, but that though this be so, yet we are not alone for our Father is with us. We are pilgrims, our life is a long walk, a journey from earth to heaven."[1]

After rambling for a bit about what it meant to be a pilgrim, van Gogh eventually turned his attention to his text for the day, just four lines from the sixth chapter of Paul's second letter to the Corinthians:

> Our nature is sorrowful but for those who have learnt and are learning to look at Jesus Christ there is always reason to rejoice. It is a good word, that of St Paul: As being *sorrowful yet always rejoicing*. For those who believe in Jesus Christ there is no death and no sorrow that is not mixed with hope.[2]

Not too bad for a beginner.

Vincent felt so good about the sermon afterward that he sent the manuscript to his brother Theo with this comment: "When I stood in the pulpit I felt like someone emerging from a dark, underground vault into the friendly daylight, and it's a wonderful thought that from now on, wherever I go, I'll be preaching the gospel."[3]

Yes, it was a wonderful thought indeed—that he might spend the rest of his life working as a pastor preaching the gospel of Jesus Christ—but it wasn't meant to be. After working a couple of years as a lay pastor, making huge sacrifices to pursue his dream—giving away all his belongings and sleeping on floors— van Gogh was eventually told he was unfit for ministry.

Ironically, the Bible verse "sorrowful, yet always rejoicing" appeared no less than fifteen times in his letters during this period. One might wonder if van Gogh considered it his life verse. Oddly, though, after his termination the phrase quietly disappeared from his everyday vocabulary, only to emerge as the overarching theme in what van Gogh is known for today, his paintings. Thankfully there's more than one way to preach.

Art, like church work, was another van Gogh family business. Vincent's uncle was an art dealer, as was his brother Theo. Though Vincent may not have been a natural businessman like them, he did have natural artistic talent, which he recognized in himself when he sketched miners and peasants in his free time during his work as a lay pastor.

With no other viable employment paths available, Vincent decided to pursue his only option. In 1881 van Gogh moved back to the Netherlands and dedicated himself to becoming an artist, made possible because of his brother Theo's financial and emotional support. Van Gogh continued this arrangement— Theo paying his bills and Vincent sending him his paintings to sell—until his untimely death ten years later.

To read the correspondence between van Gogh and his brother during that period is simply heartbreaking. If there ever was another person besides the apostle Paul who embodied the words "sorrowful, yet always rejoicing," it was van Gogh.

Vincent came out of the gate with unbridled enthusiasm for learning his craft: "I'm drawing a great deal and think it's getting better."[4]

On other occasions, however, we see him questioning whether what he was doing would ever have any aesthetic or financial value: "It is a gloomy enough prospect to have to say to myself that perhaps the painting I am doing will never be of any value whatever. If it was worth what it cost to do, I could say, 'I never bothered my head about money.' But as things are, on the contrary it absorbs me."[5]

One can't help but feel for van Gogh when reading how he talked about himself as his art didn't get recognized by his peers: "There may be a great fire in our soul, and no one ever comes to warm himself at it; the passers-by see only a little bit of smoke coming through the chimney, and pass on their way."[6] Despite these periods of intense self-doubt, van Gogh tried to stay hopeful: "I am still far from being what I want to be, but with God's help I shall succeed."[7]

Most of his days were spent shuffling between discouragement and absolute despair, especially in his final years. Unlike artists like Rembrandt, who were discovered early and paid enormous commissions to paint for wealthy aristocrats and royalty, giving them near instant notoriety, van Gogh toiled for a decade without ever catching a break.

History has had a much kinder view of van Gogh.

After only ten years, his flurry of artistic activity left an *immense* body of work—over nine hundred paintings in all—compared to Rembrandt's three paintings produced over nearly four decades.

The truly ironic thing is that van Gogh's paintings and drawings are on display in museums around the world, yet he died thinking that he was a failure. He never sold his paintings to more than a handful of buyers.

Maybe that's because of bad luck.

Maybe that's because he never got a break early on as Rembrandt did.

Maybe that's because his brother Theo was not that great of a salesman.

Or maybe that's because some sermons take twenty minutes to write, while others take a lifetime.

IN THE VALLEY

I have a friend who is an aspiring country music artist. He's an exceptional singer and performer, and I've known many. He's as talented as any of the people who top the Billboard charts. But despite all of his hard work, he just hasn't gotten a break. He works at Costco during the day and plays whatever small gigs he can get at night. He's been doing this for years.

I have another friend who lost his job as a pastor, and since he didn't want to move his family out of the area, he took a job making horseradish in a food processing plant. For ten hours a day, he prepared horseradish instead of sermons.

I have another friend who hasn't been able to get a teaching job. She's interviewed and interviewed for over a decade. Not a year. A *decade!* Nothing has materialized. Schools in her area just aren't hiring, and since she and her husband don't feel like

God wants them to move, she works part-time at a small Christian elementary school.

Now, for some, working at a food processing plant is a dream come true. Working at Costco is noble work that one should be proud of. Teaching at a Christian elementary school is an admirable calling.

But not if you feel drawn by providence to do something else.

Here's a scary question: *What if my friends didn't get where they are by accident? What if God placed them in those situations?*

When we pray for God's favor, what if sometimes the only way for him to *truly* bless us is to place us in total obscurity for a season? Being hidden from the view of the crowd, tucked away in some secret crevasse of the world, would have a way of teaching us lessons that popularity and success cannot.

This is the kind of thing that makes those accustomed to celebrating overnight-success stories bristle.

Obscurity is a word formed from two Latin words: *ob* (over) and *scurus* (covered). *Obscurus* in Latin means "dark," as in when the sun is "covered over" in a rainstorm.[8]

Haven't you noticed that three things tend to get "covered over" when we find ourselves wasting away in obscurity: recognition, opportunity, and self-worth?

Recognition. One of the most painful parts of obscurity is that people don't recognize the gifts and talents we have. We feel undervalued. We were created for so much more, but for some reason people can't see it.

Opportunity. Next, doors keep getting slammed in our faces. It is always other people—less talented, less committed, and less whatever—who seem to keep getting the lucky breaks. If obscurity is driving the car, comparison is always riding shotgun.

Self-worth. Second-guessing ourselves is perhaps the most excruciating byproduct of tours of duty in obscurity. Trying to beat down doors while watching others waltz through them has a way of overturning the self-worth apple cart.

When people tell us to "hang in there" because our time is coming, their well-intended words only add fuel to the fire. Our time never seems to come, and we assume we know the real reason: we're not as good as we think we are. Otherwise, why else would we be stuck?

The entire witness of Scripture leads to one inescapable conclusion on this matter: obscurity is a sign of God's favor, not a sign of his anger.

Thankfully, there is a good reason God sends people like me, you, and van Gogh into obscurity. You're not going to like the answer, but it is somewhat comforting to know one exists.

Here it is, courtesy of Oswald Chambers: "God gives us the vision, then he takes us down to the valley to batter us into the shape of the vision, and it is in the valley that so many of us faint and give way. Every vision will be made real if we will have patience."[9]

God places us in obscure places and situations because we're not ready yet. Our spiritual maintenance lights are on. Outside forces must be brought to bear to shape us into the kind of people who can handle the vision we've been given. Until that happens, doors remain shut. This happens because

God knows that without the valley, the vision will never come to fruition.

Let's be honest: it's hard to focus on what God wants if we depend on getting *recognition* from those around us to stay motivated, isn't it?

It's hard to rely on God when doors of *opportunity* seem to open by themselves.

And it's undeniably difficult to take the hits, comments, pushback, and outright opposition that comes as we pursue God's vision for our lives if our self-worth is rooted in what other people say about us.

If recognition, opportunity, and self-worth are stirred up into the fuel that drives our culture, then the valley is God's opportunity to flush that unholy concoction out of our exhaust. God-sized dreams are never driven, nor sustained, by worldly ambitions.

God has a vision for how each of our lives will turn out. He has a series of meaningful and weighty assignments that we're called to accomplish. Unfortunately, more often than not the training for *how to handle* those assignments doesn't usually happen until *after* they're handed to us.

So if you have been asking for God's favor on your life, and he has "blessed" you by giving you a dream, but

~ doors have been shut,

~ emails have gone unreturned,

~ applications have been turned down,

~ and calls have gone unanswered,

even though you've

~ tried everything,

~ prayed everything,

~ given everything,

~ and sacrificed everything,

then hang on. You're exactly where God wants you to be right now.

Just ask Joseph.

HERE COMES THE DREAMER

In her book *Daring Greatly*, author Brené Brown argues that contemporary culture breeds within people a "fear of being ordinary."[10] Raised watching reality TV shows with their incessant celebrity worship, we can understand why. Here, before us is an ordinary person like me, adored by millions.

The problem is worsened by near nonstop access to social media platforms, which steadily communicate that our real worth is measured by the number of "likes" we receive by our peers.

We grow up expecting others to confirm to us that we matter. That we're important. That what we're doing makes a difference in the grand scheme of things. We crave just one more follower, one more like, just one more person commenting on how funny, interesting, and pretty we are. Because if other people say it is so, then it is so. We are genuinely afraid of being average.

The story of Joseph is interesting because it turns that logic on its head. It shows us that one of the greatest blessings God can favor us with is not answering our prayers to make us successful, but freeing us from the need to be successful altogether. For Joseph, like all of us, that only happens in the valley.

The story begins in Genesis 37:2, where we're told, "Joseph, a young man of seventeen, was tending the flocks with his brothers." That's about the age of a typical high school senior, right at the juncture when they're wondering what will become of their life.

God confirmed that he indeed had a plan for him. Genesis 37:5 simply says, "Joseph had a dream."

It always begins with a dream, doesn't it? Literally or figuratively, we all need a picture that helps explain where we're headed. We all need a roadmap to find the place where, as Frederick Buechner says, our "deep gladness and the world's deep hunger meet."[11]

Joseph actually was given two dreams, but with the same message. In one he dreamed that eleven tightly bound bundles of grain bowed down to one solitary sheave in an act of submission. In the other, celestial bodies left their heavenly orbits in the sky and placed themselves at the feet of single star. To Joseph, the symbolism was both striking and clear: eventually, his eleven brothers would all bow down and serve him.

I bet Joseph wished he never opened his mouth to share those dreams with his brothers. Telling your eleven brothers they would serve you one day was grounds for giving you a head swirly in the toilet, or worse.

There's a deeper reason, however, to be cautious how and with whom we share God's dreams for our lives. Seeking help to *clarify* a dream God has given us is quite helpful. Seeking *affirmation*, particularly of the wrong people, can be deadly. We're led to believe that it was in tones of youthful pride that Joseph first shared his God-ordained future.

"Here comes that dreamer!" they said to each other. "Come now, let's kill him" (Genesis 37:19-20).

In what surely began as a prank that went one step too far, Joseph was thrown into a cistern and then sold off to slave traders heading to Egypt. The brothers told their father he had been killed, and offered Joseph's treasured coat dipped in animal blood to make the story believable.

Thus began a thirteen-year odyssey of obscurity for the seventeen-year-old Joseph.

Once in Egypt Joseph was sold to a police officer named Potiphar, who managed the security detail for Pharaoh's palace. It was there—away from his family and everything he had ever known—that Joseph let his dream quietly fade away. Behind the scenes, however, God was just getting started.

"The LORD was with Joseph so that he prospered," we're told, and "when his master saw that the LORD was with him and that the LORD gave him success in everything he did, Joseph found favor in his eyes and became his attendant" (Genesis 39:2-4).

Out on his own, blessed by God's favor, Joseph was forced to realize leadership gifts that he never saw in himself. Unfortunately, Joseph wasn't the only one who saw something in him. Potiphar's wife, gazing at him from a distance, seized the opportunity to use him sexually, an advance he quickly rebuffed.

Humiliated, she falsely accused him of assault, a charge that
landed him in prison.

4,725 DAYS TO OVERNIGHT SUCCESS

Valleys come in different shapes and sizes—first a cistern, now
a prison—but they all feel the same.

We don't know how long he was incarcerated, but we do
know that God didn't abandon him. "While Joseph was there
in prison, the LORD was with him; he showed him kindness
and granted him favor in the eyes of the prison warden"
(Genesis 39:20-21).

As in Potiphar's household, Joseph rose to a position of
leadership. We're even told that Joseph was made responsible
for "all that was done" in prison. "The warden paid no attention to anything under Joseph's care, because the LORD
was with Joseph and gave him success in whatever he did"
(Genesis 39:23).

Isn't it interesting how God can give us a dream and then
lead us to the valley to be trained to fulfill that dream? Given
multiple options, no one in their right mind would choose the
one that leads through the valley. I guess that's why the route
is sometimes chosen for us.

Fortunately for Joseph, while God's original vision for his
life seemed out of reach, he developed a knack for helping
others discern the dream God had for them. Pharaoh's cupbearer, who held the same kind of position as Nehemiah
did, was thrown into prison for offending Pharaoh. In a
dungeon of despair, the cupbearer's dream was interpreted
by Joseph.

Philip Yancey said, "I have learned that faith means trusting in advance what will only make sense in reverse."[12] This was certainly the case for Joseph; that small act of kindness shown to the cupbearer years later became the very act that landed Joseph an audience with the most powerful man on the planet (see Genesis 41).

One day, Pharaoh had a disturbing dream and shared it with the cupbearer, who had since been released from prison. The cupbearer recalled that while in prison he met a man who spoke personally with the gods.

"Now a young Hebrew was there with us," he told Pharaoh, "a servant of the captain of the guard. We told him our dreams, and he interpreted them for us, giving each man the interpretation of his dream."

Pharaoh immediately sent for Joseph.

Standing before a man the whole world considered a god had to be a frightening thing for a poor shepherd boy turned slave turned convict. The height of the columns and gold-laden corridors must have surely seemed other-worldly to Joseph.

"I had a dream," Pharaoh said to Joseph, "and no one can interpret it."

Joseph's quick, unfiltered response was the kind that comes only after spending years in a valley. It was a decidedly different response than the one he would have given thirteen years earlier before time and despondency had shaped his character.

"I cannot do it," Joseph replied to Pharaoh, "but God will give Pharaoh the answer he desires."

In one dream Pharaoh saw seven fat cows getting eaten by seven lean ones. In another Pharaoh dreamed that seven heads of healthy grain were devoured by seven emaciated ones.

"I told this to the magicians," Pharaoh told Joseph, "but none of them could explain it to me."

"God has shown Pharaoh what he is about to do," Joseph immediately shot back.

Pharaoh's kingdom was to experience seven years of agricultural abundance unlike any other, followed by seven years of famine no one could imagine. In the wake of the oncoming drought, the one man who had the power to prepare his country to survive, had to act.

"Now let Pharaoh look for a discerning and wise man and put him in charge of the land of Egypt," Joseph said. This man would lead the effort of collecting and storing a fifth of the harvest each year for seven years, to prepare Egypt for the hard times to come.

We're led to assume that Joseph was just as shocked as anyone when Pharaoh pointed his finger right back at him and told him he knew the perfect man for the job.

"Can we find anyone like this man, one in whom is the spirit of God?"

Then in one of the most ironic statements ever written in the entire Bible, we're told, "Joseph was thirty years old when he entered the service of Pharaoh king of Egypt."

Joseph—the shepherd boy, sold off by his brothers, falsely accused, languishing in prison, forgotten by both time and family, wasting away in utter and complete obscurity—finds himself elevated to the second-highest position in the land.

More than a decade after his brothers threw him into a pit they came to Egypt seeking grain. They did not know it was Joseph they appeared before, and so the dream God gave Joseph was fulfilled, exactly the way he saw it as a seventeen-year-old boy. His brothers all bowed down to him.

Catherine Marshall observed, "Dreams carried around in one's heart for years, if they are dreams that have God's approval, have a way of suddenly materializing."[13]

That's just as true for you as it was for Joseph.

ALWAYS REJOICING

Can I ask you a question I probably already know the answer to?

What if God in his wisdom doesn't want you to experience success in the eyes of your peers? I mean, what if the true impact of your life—the real reason you were put on this planet—was to impact someone generations after your death?

What if like van Gogh, God doesn't intend for you to experience worldly success during your lifetime? Would you be content with that?

I said I probably already know the answer, because if you were to ask me that same question, I would answer no, I'm *not* content with not experiencing success.

Deep down inside, there's something that still yearns for worldly validation. This probably explains why I keep walking out of one valley only to walk right back into another one. I've come a long way, but occasionally my "fear of being ordinary" maintenance light still blinks.

I think what God is ultimately trying to teach me and you through obscurity is that as long as he calls us his children, we'll never be simply average. In the same way the children of English royalty bypass lines and rub shoulders with the world's power brokers—not based on anything they've done, but because of whose they are, you and I are powerful beyond imagination. We're successful beyond anything the world can offer. Our every move is followed by countless angelic beings. Jesus has invited us to join him center stage in God's grand story.

Not only are we granted the privilege of knowing God in an intimate way, but we get to walk *with* him, obey his commands, follow him, carry out his purposes, and celebrate his victories. Who cares how many temporary "likes" we get or how many fleeting accolades we receive from our peers? There is nothing this world can offer that ranks any higher than being placed on the VIP list of people God intimately knows and speaks to on a regular basis.

When we find ourselves in valleys of obscurity, we must view success not as the world views it but as God does. If you're a follower of Jesus, you are *already* successful in the eyes of the only person who matters. It is impossible for you to be ordinary. You have nothing left to prove.

Trying to find validation of your self-worth through your friends, work associates, family, and perfect strangers will take you further away from the one thing you were created to do. "Find out what pleases the Lord," the apostle Paul encourages us in Ephesians 5:10. That should be our only concern.

This is why when obscurity knocks on our door, we should rush to pack our bags. Each day spent out of the limelight moves us one step closer to more effectively casting the limelight on him.

Will you make mistakes? Will you struggle with accepting this aspect of God's favor when you've prayed for success? Will you secretly wish other people do poorly so you can appear more important in people's eyes? Of course. Godliness takes a long time to take shape; or, in the words of my friend Bill, "Some sermons take twenty minutes to write. Others take a lifetime."

God may in fact exalt you to *exactly* where you wanted to go in the first place, but if that happens, your time in the valley will have taught you that success neither validates your worth nor diminishes the worth of others.

So until God has etched the last word in the grand story he is preaching through your life, allow yourself to be *sorrowful* at times, for times will be hard for sure, but never forget to be *always rejoicing.*

FIVE

SUPERNATURAL PROVISION

We don't believe something by merely saying we believe it,
or even when we believe that we believe it.
We believe something when we act as if it were true.

DALLAS WILLARD, *RENOVATION OF THE HEART*

EVERYONE KNOWS THAT IF YOU ASK two dads with Type A personalities to colead their kids' first-grade class Halloween party, they're probably going to get into a fist fight.

I knew there was going to be trouble when I showed up with my grocery-store cupcakes in clear plastic containers with the white price sticker on top and my coleader walked in carrying large white bakery boxes with bright orange bows on them.

Oh, okay, so this is how it's gonna be, I thought to myself.

This dad reminded me of a goofy, flamboyant character on a sitcom. He wore a blue sport coat with a beige sweater underneath, had dyed his hair jet black, and used exaggerated mannerisms. He went around and made sure to hug every kid in the class and tell them how special they were.

It was touch and go there for a while to see who the cooler dad was going to be. At first, it looked like I was one-upped by the cupcakes. His were twice as large as mine *and* had rainbow sprinkles.

Fortunately, I made a comeback when the games began. We each were to come prepared to lead three games. He went first and struggled out of the gate. I knew he'd hit a roadblock. The good news is that my time spent as a youth-ministry intern years prior taught me the two time-tested rules of successful games for kids: *make it competitive and make it gross.* When I saw that he was losing their attention, I saw my chance and stepped in.

"Kids, I have some games I'd like us to play. Let's start with a game that's similar to pin the tail on the donkey, but with a twist. It's called 'Walk blindfolded toward your friend who is standing with their back against the wall and try to smash a cupcake in their face.'"

The kids thought the game was great. Mrs. White, however, my daughter's teacher, not so much. Apparently, cupcakes leave stains on chalkboards.

While I'll admit the chalkboard was unfortunate collateral damage, what really mattered was there were no fisticuffs, and I went from class zero to class hero in a matter of minutes.

After we finished cleaning up, the teacher told me (and I quote), "Thank you, Mr. Jones, for what had to be the most *interesting* class party in my twenty-eight-year teaching career."

A few weeks later my daughter got an invitation to a birthday party for a boy in her class. I didn't recognize the name, but since I knew where the family lived based on the address on the invitation, I agreed to take her. They were in first grade, so it was still a "come and stay with your kid" kind of party, instead of drop off and leave.

Cars lined the street, forcing us to walk a bit to get to the house. We went to the front door first, but no one answered. The laughter and giggling coming out of the backyard told us we should just walk back.

As we turned the corner, I was shocked. I thought we had accidentally stumbled into a circus! There was a face painter, a balloon lady, an inflatable bounce house, tables full of catered food, and streamers and inflatable balloons everywhere. In all my years as a young parent, I had never seen anything like it.

What the heck? I thought. *This is ridiculous. The kid is a first grader, for crying out loud.*

My mind immediately went to how my daughter's last birthday party paled by comparison.

"There he is!" my daughter said, as she ran over to meet the birthday boy. Behind him, as luck would have it, stood you-know-who.

Well of course. Of course! Now this party makes perfect sense, I mumbled to myself.

"Hey, great to see you again," I told him half-heartedly.

"We're *so* glad you could make it," he said. "Please make yourself comfortable and . . ." he stopped mid-sentence and quickly grabbed a kid, lifting her up into the air right before she ran into another parent.

I spent the next forty-five minutes following my daughter around to the different activities. The dad pretty much did the same thing with his son, except he had a camera in hand, as did the two sets of grandparents and his wife. They looked like paparazzi following a movie star.

When it came time to open gifts, he exploded with excitement as each one was opened. His reaction was the same with every gift: animated clapping followed by high-fiving his son.

After all the gifts had been unwrapped, the dad called everyone's attention to a large, unwrapped gift sitting next to the food table. It was a go-cart—arguably the coolest gift ever for a first-grade boy.

Well, of course, I said to myself. *What's next? Spaceship rides?*

As I stood there trying to wrap my mind around all of this—watching the grandparents snap pictures and the mom scurrying about making sure she knew who each kid was that gave each gift—I noticed something I didn't pick up on before.

The grandparents were old. Like *really* old. Then I looked over at the dad and thought, *I wonder how old he is?*

I quickly added things up in my mind: bakery-fresh cupcakes *plus* dressing up in a blazer to go to a class party *plus* dyed black hair *plus* parents in their late forties *plus* elderly grandparents plus a son who didn't look like either mom or dad *equals* ohh!

Maybe they couldn't have kids. Maybe they adopted. He's their only one.

What I was watching took on a whole new perspective. I spent the rest of the party watching him watch his son. Perhaps years of infertility treatments and failed adoptions had a way of giving this couple an insight most of us don't have about what an absolute never-to-be-taken-for-granted privilege it is to be given children to raise.

His overly expressive mannerisms didn't bother me anymore. I could see the innocent exuberance behind the go-cart. I understood the countless pictures. It made perfect sense why they were willing to blow that kind of cash on a six-year-old's birthday party.

Sometimes it takes seeing ourselves through the eyes of a new parent to catch a glimpse of what it must be like for God to look at us from heaven.

ASK, SEEK, KNOCK

Jesus taught that if you ever wondered whether God wants to intervene in your life to give you a blessing, all you have to do is think of the craziest, most over-the-top, sitting-on-the-edge-of-his-seat-with-anticipation, ready-to-shower-you-with-amazing-gifts type of dad, like that father at the party, then multiply that a thousandfold.

We know this because at the end of the Sermon on the Mount Jesus taught, "Ask and it will be given to you; seek and you will find; knock and the door will be opened to you. For everyone who asks receives; the one who seeks finds; and to the one who knocks, the door will be opened" (Matthew 7:7-8).

That's an open, unrestricted promise, with no fine print. You ask, God intervenes, period. No hesitation. No qualification. No ambiguity. God does.

When I say God wants to intervene in your life, let me be absolutely clear what I'm talking about: I mean God actually wants to enter our time-space continuum and alter minds, hearts, physical bodies, events, atmospheric conditions, political systems, people groups, and anything else that is a part of the material universe so he can accomplish his purpose in your life.

Yes, I'm talking about what we call miracles.

But not just big miracles. Everyday ones. Remember, Jesus was talking to people like you and me when he first delivered those words. This wasn't a philosophical discussion for him.

God is in the intervention business. He wants to intervene in your marriage. He wants to intervene in your kid's third-grade teacher's crappy attitude because it is causing your child so much self-doubt.

He wants to intervene in your job search, your health scare, your problems with your neighbors, your car situation, your corporate deal that is causing you so much stress, and your staggering tuition bill that is looming.

Do you believe God wants to intervene in your life like this?

I know you probably believe he *can* do things like this, as in that it is theoretically possible. I didn't ask that. I asked if you thought God *does* things like this. Like *actually* intervenes in direct response to our prayers.

Before you respond by saying, "I've tried asking God to intervene in my life and nothing happened," look at what Jesus said right after he told people to ask and seek:

> Which of you, if your son asks for bread, will give him a
> stone? Or if he asks for a fish, will give him a snake? If

you, then, though you are evil, know how to give good gifts to your children, how much more will your Father in heaven give good gifts to those who ask him! (Matthew 7:9-11)

No human parent, Jesus says, is going to play tricks on their kid when they're hungry. This may not seem like that powerful of an example to us, but it certainly was to the people Jesus was talking to who lived hand to mouth. They didn't know where their next meal was coming from. If your kid is starving, and you hand them a rock, and they bite into it, that's a pretty evil act.

More than likely you're not starving, but you've probably bitten into your fair share of rocks. You've bitten into a job you thought would be life-giving, and it broke a few teeth. You've tried having children but couldn't, and while others are carrying babies, you feel like you're carrying a boulder in your heart. If you've gone through the pain of divorce, you can probably write a book on the perils of marrying a snake.

HOW MUCH MORE?

So let me ask again: Do you believe God really intervenes in our lives?

Studies have shown that the more educated you are, the less likely you are to believe in an "interventionist deity." I take these kinds of studies with a grain of salt because surveys have also shown that the more educated you are, the more likely you are to *avoid* watching reruns of the zombie TV show *The Walking Dead*, the single greatest cinematic achievement of the twenty-first century. But I digress.

If you are educated, there are probably a dozen good reasons why you might think God's intervention is a ridiculous idea, and I'll probably agree with most of them.

The thing I want you to consider, however, is that Jesus taught that our heavenly Father performs miracles—and they aren't some sleight-of-hand trick on a televangelist's stage either.

Theologian D. A. Carson argued that what is at stake in Matthew 7 is a person's understanding of the nature of God. He writes,

> God must not be thought of as … a malicious tyrant who takes vicious glee in tricks he plays (vv. 9-10), or even as an indulgent grandfather who provides everything requested of him. He is the heavenly Father, the God of the kingdom, who graciously and willingly bestows the good gifts of the kingdom in answer to prayer.[1]

If you struggle with thinking God might act like that father at the party, I want you to notice three other words Jesus spoke: *how much more.*

Those unfamiliar with the religious context in which Jesus taught might not be aware that what he is doing is attacking our objections about God by using a rhetorical technique commonly used by rabbis of his time.

When Jesus was a young child, the most popular rabbi in Israel was Hillel (110 BC to AD 10). Hillel is considered one of the most influential teachers in all of Jewish history. Some scholars wonder if the story in Luke's Gospel about Jesus' parents losing him in Jerusalem and finding him days later in the temple "sitting among the teachers, listening to them and asking them questions" (Luke 2:41-46) is an allusion to Jesus meeting Hillel. Luke said, "Everyone who heard him was amazed at his understanding and his answers" (Luke 2:47). Whether or not Jesus actually met Hillel, we know Jesus learned how to debate from Hillel's techniques.

One of Hillel's strategies for proving points about God was called Qal Wahomer, which when translated from Hebrew into English means "light to heavy."[2]

Basically, if you were debating someone about God and wanted to prove a point, a light-to-heavy argument would take something small that everyone agrees on and prove that if something applies to that smaller situation, it would certainly apply to God. You know when you're dealing with a light-to-heavy argument when you see the words "how much more."

Like all great rabbis, the apostle Paul used the principle of light to heavy (how much more) when he tried to prove his points about Jesus:

> Since we have now been justified by his blood, *how much more* shall we be saved from God's wrath through him! For if, while we were God's enemies, we were reconciled to him through the death of his Son, *how much more*, having been reconciled, shall we be saved through his life! (Romans 5:9-10)

Elsewhere we see Jesus himself using the principle of light to heavy (how much more) when attacking the Pharisees for critiquing him for performing miracles on the Sabbath: "If any of you has a sheep and if it falls into a pit on the Sabbath, will you not take hold of it and lift it out? *How much more* valuable is a person than a sheep? Therefore it is lawful to do good on the Sabbath" (Matthew 12:11-12).

The sabbath-sheep-pit illustration is a perfect example of using light to heavy (how much more) to prove a point. Jesus picked a smaller thing that everyone considered valuable (a sheep) and compared that to something the Pharisees didn't agree on as being valuable (human beings in pain on the sabbath).

Understanding light to heavy (how much more) helps us understand what Jesus was trying to do in Matthew 7:

Ask and it will be given to you; seek and you will find; knock and the door will be opened to you. For everyone who asks receives; the one who seeks finds; and to the one who knocks, the door will be opened.

Which of you, if your son asks for bread, will give him a stone? Or if he asks for a fish, will give him a snake? If you, then, though you are evil, know how to give good gifts to your children, *how much more* will your Father in heaven give good gifts to those who ask him! (Matthew 7:7-11)

Jesus said that if parents like you and me and the over-the-top cupcake guy are evil (compared to God), but we still know how to give good gifts to our kids, *how much more* will God give us good gifts if we just ask!

Jesus' point is that God wants to intervene in our everyday lives just as powerfully and miraculously as he did in the Bible. God has not changed in the least.

What has changed is our expectation of what he is capable of doing, and our understanding of how he goes about doing it.

FAVOR IN THE PSALMS

What specific prayer do you need answered right now? Whatever it is, I encourage you to ask God to grant you his favor and specifically grant you your request. But I must warn you: Praying for God's favor is the single most dangerous prayer anyone can pray. That's because God rarely gives us *exactly* what we want, but he always gives us what we need.

We need to understand that sometimes he *does* give us *exactly* what we want.

Sometimes when we pray for something we need in our lives, he supernaturally provides for that need, exactly as we prayed for it.

Miraculously.

Dramatically.

Decidedly.

We need to allow ourselves to expect God to occasionally respond like that when we pray for his favor.

I love how the writers of the psalms innocently pray for God's favor, and then expect that they'll receive the "good gifts" that they're praying for:

> But I pray to you, LORD,
>> in the time of your favor;
> in your great love, O God,
>> answer me with your sure salvation. (Psalm 69:13)

For the LORD God is a sun and shield;
   the LORD bestows favor and honor;
no good thing does he withhold
   from those whose walk is blameless. (Psalm 84:11)

May the favor of the Lord our God rest on us;
   establish the work of our hands for us—
   yes, establish the work of our hands. (Psalm 90:17)

One of the scariest things about living in the wake of creepy TV evangelists and health-and-wealth preachers is that we've swung so far in the opposite direction of not expecting God to answer our prayers that we're shocked when he does.

A. W. Tozer wrote, "What comes into our minds when we think about God is the most important thing about us. . . . We tend by a secret law of the soul to move toward our mental image of God."[3]

Who do you picture when you close your eyes to pray? The God represented by the father who gives their kid a rock or bread? A fish or a snake?

If you don't expect God to give you gifts, that's a problem.

If you don't expect good gifts, that's an *even bigger* problem.

Listen, I get it, there have been times when you've prayed for a certain thing to happen, and it didn't happen exactly the way you thought it would. Later, we'll talk more about the kind of favor God granted you in that particular situation.

But you need to understand that a war is being fought over your mind, and whoever wins that battle, the battle over who you think God is and what you think God can and will do will control how you live your life.

Many Christians take what they know to be true about the way their life works and try to make God fit into that first. Jesus teaches us to do the exact opposite. We're to get absolute clarity on who God is and what he wants to do in our lives first, then we're to make our experience fit into God's reality.

This is essential because, as Tozer points out, our experience of God will end up conforming to our image of God.

INNOCENT FAITH

I'm naturally a skeptical person, even though I've been a pastor for over a quarter of a century now.

I want to be honest with you: I wrestle with this aspect of God's favor. Partly because I don't want to come across as a religious kook. But also because we live in a culture that undermines the confidence of people who believe in a deity that grants miraculous answers to prayer.

Not coincidentally, God had to take me to one of the most remote places left on this planet to teach me that he truly is the good Father Jesus talked about in Matthew 7.

He did it through an elderly fisherman who had never gone to school, never placed his hands under running water, never flipped a light switch.

He spoke only two words; yet I've never forgotten them.

For years I had felt convicted that we as a church weren't actively pursuing people far from God to "the ends of the earth" (Acts 1:8). As the senior pastor of an evangelistic church that has led thousands of people to faith in Jesus, our church had not yet ventured out internationally besides short-term mission trips to Haiti and Mexico.

I called a friend who leads an organization that plants churches among the least-reached people left on earth.

"We want to go to the most unreached place left on the planet," I told him. "Someplace no one else is willing to go."

"I know just the place," he said. "But it's going to be a challenge."

He told me about an unreached region in Southeast Asia with over a million people who had never had a Christian step within their villages.

"It's illegal for us to go there, but we have a man on the ground that I met last year. He's started a small church with no resources. He's our inroad."

Six months later three of us were in the air to meet this local church planter and see the possibilities for ourselves. Unfortunately, to protect our team's identity on the ground, I can't tell you where this place is. The pressure on the new converts to leave their new faith in Jesus is fierce.

After an eighteen-hour flight, followed by another four-hour flight, followed by a six-hour drive on some of the worst roads I've ever driven on, a night's stay in a hostel, then a two-hour bone-jarring jeep ride through the wilderness, we peeked through the canopy cover and saw a small village on the horizon.

As we drove closer, a little boy ran out to meet us and ran beside our car, laughing the entire way in. Women working in the fields dropped what they were doing, and within minutes we were encircled by some of the most joyous people I have ever met.

When our local missionary introduced us, they clapped. We were the first Westerners that had ever visited their village. Children grabbed us by the hand as they took us on a tour.

As we walked through their fields and went into their huts, I was struck by how completely cut off from the outside world they were. All they had was the rice they grew from the soil. *Difficult* is too soft of a word to describe what they had to endure just to survive. Their laughter reminded me of the way the apostle Paul described leaders in the early church, "having nothing, and yet possessing everything" (2 Corinthians 6:9-10).

Eventually, they took us to a small bamboo church building that had recently been erected in the center of the village. We could hear their singing and clapping from some distance away. The song leader smiled and nodded as we walked in and took our place among the eighty-plus new converts that had come to Jesus in the last two years.

Their passion was euphoric. In between the heartfelt songs, all newly written by people in the village, these believers shared stories of God's faithfulness and protection. One man shared how God had enabled him to be generous with another non-believing family in need. A woman shared how God had completely healed her child of a life-threatening sickness—all the more urgent, I discovered, since the village is an arduous three days' journey from the hospital through mountains with roaming tigers, leopards, and elephants.

We were humbled as they asked us to speak, then presented us with gifts. Afterward, to our absolute surprise and delight, they took us by the hand to a bamboo hut where the entire village had come together to prepare a feast.

They placed bamboo leaves before us, and one by one villagers placed food before us. Honestly, I didn't know what half of the stuff was, but our church planter told us that this was more food than any person in the village would eat in two weeks, so I kept eating.

And then it happened.

Into the hut walked a man with stalks of bamboo in his arms. He walked up to each of us, turned the bamboo stalks upside down, and small fish plopped onto our makeshift plates. They were delicious. They had been seasoned and cooked over an open fire inside the bamboo stalks.

"Where did you get these?" I asked our translator to ask him.

"Earlier today," he told us, "I went to the river and prayed that God would allow me to catch your meal tonight."

Then he raised his head and hands to the sky, laughed, and shouted something toward the sky. He then looked back at me with a wide grin.

Our interpreter saw that I was looking for him to translate what he just said.

"'God provided!' he says."

We all smiled and nodded in agreement.

The food continued to be brought out. Questions by my friends were asked. New faces kept entering the hut.

Meanwhile, I sat frozen, looking at the man, overtaken by the audacity of his faith, unmarred by twenty-five years of "education" in the West. I sat entranced, just staring at him, convicted of my idolatrous skepticism and speechless in the presence of someone who knew the Lord I had spent so many years only studying.

"Let us remove the ignorance and darkness that spreads like a mist over our sight," argued the second-century writer Clement of Alexandria, "and let us get a vision of the true God."[4]

Sometimes God, the God of the Bible, the real God, the God my friend knows, delights in bestowing his favor on us by giving good gifts, exactly the way we ask for them.

That's because the same Jesus who miraculously provided fish for his disciples almost two thousand years ago is still providing fish for people today.

SIX

BODILY AFFLICTION

I have pain, but I have peace, I have peace.

RICHARD BAXTER, *SELECT PRACTICAL WRITINGS*

BETWEEN THE AGES OF EIGHTEEN AND FORTY-TWO, I could count on one hand the number of times I went to the doctor.

But when I turned forty-three, for no apparent reason, I developed a severe neurological condition that triggered nonstop debilitating pain in the back-left base of my head. I went to three different specialists, and they were all baffled. Unable to find a cause, they put me on antiseizure medication.

Over the next five years, I underwent three surgeries, five MRIs, three CAT scans, and more ultrasounds and EKGs than

I can remember. I had nine different rounds of medication administered via epidural injections in my back and neck. I lost most of the hearing in my left ear. I gained thirty pounds. I became depressed. I suffered extreme panic attacks. I went on an antidepressant. The pain became so severe that I could only sleep in forty-five-minute stretches before being jolted out of bed in pain.

My life verse throughout all of this was Job 13:15: "Though he slay me, yet I will hope in him."

My lowest point was the morning I received news from a team of neurologists (considered by many to be among the best in the United States) that there was nothing more they could do for me. Out of options, I called my family doctor, who happens to be a Christian, and he told me to come right over.

"Brian, I'm so sorry this is happening," he gently said. "How can I help you?"

"Dr. Yang, I've gone to every . . ."

My eyes filled with tears.

I buried my face in my hands.

Then I completely broke down.

Now, you have to understand that my kids claim that they've never seen me cry. And that's probably not far from the truth. Besides my two grandmothers' funerals and the middle of the movie *Forrest Gump* (spoiler alert) when Bubba dies, I can't remember losing it. I'm just not a crying kind of person.

But not this day.

I cried long enough and hard enough to make up for lost time.

Soon after this, I began seeing a Christian counselor. She told me during our first session that she has found each of us believe a core truth about how the world works, and it's usually wrong. In the vast majority of instances, these core beliefs have no basis in (1) the truth of God's Word and (2) reality itself.

She leaned toward me and asked, "Brian, what's your *core truth?*"

Without hesitation, I fired back: "That we are all completely and utterly alone."

A few weeks later a group of friends at our church gathered around me in prayer.

Throughout all of this I shared next to none of my struggles with anyone in the church besides my staff and these few men. I mention this because there's a good chance that you have friends right now experiencing immense physical or emotional pain who seem just fine. As Søren Kierkegaard observed, "Happiness is the greatest hiding place for despair."[1]

My friends approached me after a church service and said, "That's it. This is enough. We're going to anoint you with oil, pray over you, and ask God to heal you. Pick the day and time, and we'll meet you at the church."

Two days later we gathered in my office. Before they prayed they took turns reading Scripture, sharing stories about God's healing power in their lives, and how much they loved me as both their pastor and friend. To this day that was one of the kindest things anyone has ever done for me.

"What would you like the Lord to do for you?" they asked before praying.

"Mercy," I replied. "I need mercy."

Oswald Chambers tells us, "When God gets us alone through suffering, heartbreak, temptation, disappointment, sickness, or by thwarted desires, a broken friendship, or a new friendship— when He gets us absolutely alone, and we are totally speechless, unable to ask even one question, then He begins to teach us."[2]

That's what happened that night.

God didn't instantly heal me as we prayed. He did something more important. An often overlooked mystery of faith is that when we pray for *one kind* of miracle, we often receive another.

Before I went to bed that night, I randomly turned to Genesis 32. It's the story about Jacob wrestling with an angel. We're told that Jacob was so desperate that he wouldn't let the angel go. They wrestled from the middle of the night until sunrise.

The words in verse 26 leaped off the page: "I will not let you go unless you bless me."

I frantically looked to my Bible's concordance to see what else the Bible said about this event.

Looking back hundreds of years later, the prophet Hosea spoke about this incident: "He [Jacob] struggled with the angel and overcame him; he wept and begged for his favor" (Hosea 12:3-4).

Favor? I thought. *I've never heard of this. What does this mean?*

I could see myself in Jacob's shoes, and I knew that if he wanted favor bad enough that he was willing to fight God for it, and beg him for it, it must be worth having.

That next morning, I got up at 4 a.m., went down to my basement office, closed the door behind me, and told God, "I am not leaving here until you bless me."

I got up at 4 a.m. the next morning and did it again.

In fact, I began getting up at 4 a.m. every day to find and meditate on every passage in the Bible that talked about God's favor. I always finished by getting on my face before God and begging him to bless me.

I did this for over a year.

Do you want to know the stunning realization that took me a long time to figure out? The pain I was suffering at the time *was* God's blessing. The pain wasn't *keeping me* from experiencing God's favor. The pain wasn't being used by God to help me *discover* God's favor. The pain *was* God's favor.

FACING YOUR GOLIATHS

Let's take a step back and look at pain in a way you may have never thought about.

You were never meant to go to battle without the favor of God on your life. The great men and women of faith in the past understood this, which is why they sought the Lord's favor *before* they picked up their sword. With the Lord's favor the victory was ensured before the battle started. Without it, the battle was lost before it began.

So many Christians operate their lives in their own strength. They remind me of the young boy David before he became king. When the giant Goliath presented himself on the field of battle day after day, taunting the Lord's army, all the rest of the warriors cowered in fear.

David, on the other hand, heard Goliath's words and was enraged: "Who is this uncircumcised Philistine that he should defy the armies of the living God?" (1 Samuel 17:26).

Upon volunteering to fight Goliath, a task everyone considered an immediate death sentence, David was offered Saul's armor as protection, the very best in the land. But David knew that if the armor worked, every man lined up for battle that day would have worn it.

David knew a secret that few going into life's battles understand—going into battle with nothing but the favor of the Lord is better than going into battle wearing the best the world has to offer.

Walking up to Goliath with nothing more than a sling and a few stones in his hand, David vanquished the foe; the warriors routed the Philistines, and David modeled a vital lesson for us all.

Years later, David scribbled that lesson down in a song to be accompanied by flutes. It was a song about his enemies coming against him as king. "Bloodthirsty men," David called them, with hearts that were "filled with destruction." Recalling that he had faced many such foes in his life, he ended the song thinking of future generations who might sing his words:

Surely, LORD, you bless the righteous;
>   you surround them with your favor as with a shield.
>   (Psalm 5:12)

God's favor is like a full body shield, one that covered ancient warriors from head to toe. When arrows rained down so thick they blocked the sun, not a one could find its target. With this shield, no harm can come to you, unless the Lord wills it.

God's favor is like that shield. With it, you charge confidently into battle. Without it, even the best the world has to offer is not enough.

You may not consider yourself a warrior, but I beg to differ. Christians face a myriad of Goliaths in their everyday lives:

~ marriage pain

~ anxiety

~ depression

~ inability to find love

~ debt

~ loneliness

~ addictions

~ homosexual inclinations

~ discouragement

~ problems with children

~ infertility

~ lethargy

~ work that doesn't satisfy

These foes stand and mock us because we have nothing to defeat them with. No weapon of earthly origin we've tried has had a lasting effect. That's because earthly problems with spiritual causes will never be vanquished by spiritual people using earthly means alone.

Here's the thing: *sometimes sickness* is *the manifestation of God's favor.*

Let me be even clearer: your disease, that disability, the birth defect you feel ashamed of, the loss of limb or sight, cancer ravaging your body, all of it could be the physical manifestation that you are favored by God; it is the shield you are protected and blessed with.

Contrary to what you've might have been told by well-meaning Christians and pastors, and especially health-and-wealth TV evangelists, our greatest pain is often God's greatest blessing. If you've prayed for God's favor, and God has allowed you to get sick, that sickness wasn't an absence of God's favor but rather a sign of it.

The fact is for "my five years of living hell," as I called it, physical pain *was* God's blessing on my life. It *was* his favor. The pain didn't come knocking to teach me to seek God's favor. God favored me with pain, causing me to seek to understand why I had been blessed to receive it.

REALLY BAD ADVICE

One of the great tragedies of the Christian faith is that so many Christians make assumptions about why God allows suffering without actually reading what God has to say about suffering.

Nowhere is this truer than with the book of Job.

Now, to be perfectly honest, I totally get why Christians stop reading Job after a couple of chapters. It's nothing more than a compelling two-chapter introduction and a poignant four-chapter conclusion sandwiched around thirty-five of the most insufferably boring chapters written in the Bible.

Trust me, if you suffer from insomnia, read chapters 3–37 of Job. It will do the trick. Unfortunately, it is the boring middle chapters that convey the whole reason the book was written in the first place.

The book begins this way: "In the land of Uz there lived a man whose name was Job. . . . He was the greatest man among all the people of the East."

By "greatest" we're meant to understand that Job had the favor of God poured out on his life. To make sure we understand how immensely favored by God Job was, we're told two things. First, Job was wealthy. He "owned seven thousand sheep, three thousand camels, five hundred yoke of oxen and five hundred donkeys, and had a large number of servants." In a pastoral and agricultural culture, this was staggering.

Second, and probably the biggest sign of God's blessing, was the number of sons Job had. We're told, "He had seven sons and three daughters." (I have friends who have three boys. Every week I watch their poor mother walk ragged into church. Let's take it on faith that having *seven* sons is a blessing.) In a patriarchal society where a man's stature is underscored by the number of sons who can bring him wealth and security later in life, to be blessed with seven was extraordinary.

The most important thing the author of Job wants us to know is that Job's wealth and familial blessings stemmed entirely from his devotion to God. "This man was blameless and upright; he feared God and shunned evil." In fact, to help put the depth of his piety into perspective, we're told, "He was the greatest man among all the people of the East."

Job's life, however, took a sudden turn for the worse when all of these blessings were suddenly taken away from him. Marauding warriors came and stole his livestock. Fire from heaven killed his servants. Hurricane-force winds toppled a home in which all of his children were eating. In a matter of days all of Job's "blessings" were gone.

How would he respond? It would have been absolutely understandable to have blamed God for allowing these things to happen. But Job never accused God of wrongdoing, even as his body was overtaken with boils.

"Curse God and die!" Job's wife told him (Job 2:9).

Who would blame him if he did? It was clear that God had abandoned him, right? His "blessings" were gone!

"In all this," we're told, "Job did not sin in what he said" (v. 10).

The reality is we all have our own "in all this" seasons of life when it appears to everyone around us that we've been cursed. By God, by life, by karma, by Satan, by the universe—it doesn't matter who exactly—all that matters is that we seem to suffer for no apparent reason. This was me for five straight years.

Why do things like this happen to people like you, me, and Job?

The great German theologian and martyr Dietrich Bonhoeffer said that in situations "where God tears great gaps we should not try to fill them with human words."[3]

Unfortunately, Job's three friends Eliphaz, Bildad, and Zophar weren't around to listen to Bonhoeffer's advice. In their minds they knew exactly why Job was suffering and were more than willing to share that with him.

"Really Bad Advice" would be a great title for chapters 3–37 of the book. One by one, Eliphaz, Bildad, and Zophar took turns telling Job why God had cursed him and what he needed to do to be reinstated again into God's good graces.

Job's friends believed there was one simple reason Job lost his family, wealth, and health: *he sinned against God.*

It's helpful to pause for a moment and take note that the advice Job's friends gave him stemmed from an understanding of Scripture they all shared.

Eliphaz, Bildad, and Zophar committed one of the great sins of biblical interpretation—they took one small part of the Bible literally (in this case the law found in Deuteronomy) without allowing other parts of the Bible to weigh in on and shape what God said about the same topic. The reality is if we looked at Deuteronomy 28:15-24 as the *only* explanation for why people suffer, it would be easy to conclude that Job was cursed because of his sin:

> If you do not obey the LORD your God and do not carefully follow all his commands and decrees I am giving you today, all these curses will come on you and overtake you:
>
> You will be cursed in the city and cursed in the country.
>
> Your basket and your kneading trough will be cursed.
>
> The fruit of your womb will be cursed, and the crops of your land, and the calves of your herds and the lambs of your flocks.
>
> You will be cursed when you come in and cursed when you go out.
>
> The LORD will send on you curses, confusion and rebuke in everything you put your hand to, until you are destroyed and come to sudden ruin because of the evil you have done in forsaking him. The LORD will plague you with diseases until he has destroyed you from the land you are entering to possess. The LORD will strike you with wasting disease, with fever and inflammation, with scorching heat and drought, with blight and mildew, which will plague you until you perish. The sky over your head will be bronze,

the ground beneath you iron. The LORD will turn the rain
of your country into dust and powder; it will come down
from the skies until you are destroyed.

That's a pretty accurate description of what happened to Job,
wouldn't you agree?

It would appear so, if that were all God said about the issue
of suffering. No wonder Job's friends believed his suffering was
the result of his sin against God!

Look at how Eliphaz railed against Job to acknowledge
his iniquity:

Consider now: Who, being innocent, has ever perished?
    Where were the upright ever destroyed?
As I have observed, those who plow evil
    and those who sow trouble reap it. (Job 4:7-8)

Bildad piled on right after Eliphaz, trying to force Job to
see that God doesn't allow bad things to happen to good people:

Surely God does not reject one who is blameless
    or strengthen the hands of evildoers. (Job 8:20)

Even his friend Zophar pleaded with him to confess
his sins:

Yet if you devote your heart to him
    and stretch out your hands to him,
if you put away the sin that is in your hand
    and allow no evil to dwell in your tent,
then, free of fault, you will lift up your face;
    you will stand firm and without fear. (Job 11:13-15)

Eliphaz's words in Job 22:5 summarize all thirty-five chapters of their bad advice:

Is not your wickedness great?
Are not your sins endless?

Fortunately, at the end of the book, after listening to his friend's rambling counsel, God finally shows up to set the record straight:

After the LORD had said these things to Job, he said to Eliphaz the Temanite, "I am angry with you and your two friends, because you have not spoken the truth about me, as my servant Job has." (Job 42:7)

"You have not spoken the truth about me" could have been God's word to just about every Christian who tried to comfort me during my five years of turmoil.

Job wasn't suffering because of his *sin* against God. Job was suffering because of his *obedience* to God. His obedience brought him even greater levels of blessing.

Yes, you read that correctly. Losing his children was a blessing greater than having them. Losing his wealth was a blessing greater than earning it. Losing his health was a blessing greater than keeping it.

Before you swear at me and throw this book in the trash, please hear me out.

EMPTY VESSELS

The book of Job ends by telling the reader that "the LORD restored his fortunes and gave him twice as much as he had before" (Job 42:10) and that "the LORD blessed the latter part of Job's life more than the former part" (Job 42:12).

A quick reading of the ending might lead us to conclude that there were *three* distinct chapters in Job's life: the part in which he was blessed, the part in which he was cursed, and the part in which his blessings were returned.

That's exactly how Job's friends would want you to read it. Fortunately for us, the author of the book wasn't one of Job's friends or a TV evangelist or a self-help motivational speaker.

The whole point of Job, and the reason God never gives Job an answer for why he's suffering, is because *all* of Job's life was blessed—every bit of it—from the soul-numbing tragedy he endured to the embrace of his family and his staggering wealth.

How is this possibly the case? Or, to think in King David's terms, if pain is God's favor and surrounds us like a shield, what is pain shielding us from?

Job's story helps us here.

Pain shields us from living a Christian life in which we claim to know God but never actually encounter him.

The biggest blessing Job experienced wasn't his wealth or even his dear children, as much as he would have gladly given his own life to save just one of them. His greatest blessing was meeting God face to face.

In *The Imitation of Christ*, the fourteenth-century mystic Thomas à Kempis wrote, "The Lord bestows his blessings there, where he finds the vessels empty."[4]

Now, to be perfectly honest, given the choice between losing my child or getting close to God, I would choose my child every time. I don't care how holy you think you are. If you choose

God over your child there's something wrong with you, something demented, in fact. No God-honoring believer would ever willingly choose to hurt someone else to benefit themselves.

Herein lies the reason, in part, why we don't get to "choose" which kind of favor we receive when we ask God to bless us. Left to our own devices, we would only pray for the good stuff. Given the choice, we would never choose pain. The reason is that we're healthy, not that we're narcissistic.

Trust me, when Abraham took his only son Isaac to the mountain to sacrifice him on the altar, he was being tested. The test came not on the top of the mountain, but when God first asked him to do it.

MY CAR RIDE WITH FRANCIS CHAN

During my time of suffering I had a dream I'd like to share with you now.

I had a dream I was sitting in the back seat of a car, driving around the streets of 1950-ish Clearwater, Florida.

Everything I saw in my dream had a yellowish tint to it, similar to the way the Cohen brothers filmed the movie *No Country for Old Men*.

At some point in my dream, the camera angle changed, and I saw who was driving the car. Popular Christian author and speaker Francis Chan was cruising the streets past palm trees and shiny new houses.

Eventually Francis looked in the rear-view mirror and said, "I don't see it. Brian, I don't see your love for Jesus' teachings."

This is normal for Francis Chan, known for his persona of radical obedience to Scripture. I had just been listening to a podcast with Francis the day before—which is probably why he was on my mind.

Looking up from the Bible I was reading, I locked eyes with him in the mirror and defensively said, "You don't know me. You don't know me at all."

Then he pulled the car over, put it into park, and turned around.

Wiping away a single tear falling from his right eye, he said, "Brian, I'm just being honest. I just don't see it."

Then I woke up covered in sweat.

Here are three possible dream interpretations:

~ Option 1. If Francis Chan carjacks your Studebaker, remember to keep calm, and no one will get hurt. At some point he'll pull the car over and start to cry. Then you can make your move.

~ Option 2. God is calling me to move back to Clearwater, Florida (where I lived in the mid-90s), but only after everyone gets jaundice.

~ Option 3. I was having a conversation with myself—one in which I was wrestling with myself over my need to display greater levels of love for the teachings of Jesus.

I'll go with option 3.

I shared this dream with you because I want you to know that I despised the trite, formulaic "pearls of wisdom" that Christians gave me during my struggle.

The last thing I want to do is cheapen your pain by trying to throw some bow over why your spouse left you, or why you're dying of cancer, or why your child was murdered.

The last thing I want to do is make you feel better.

You don't need to feel better. You need to feel every last ounce of that pain. You must never forget. You don't need to look the other way and cover over the anger you feel toward God and the tragedy of your situation. You cannot hide from it, as you well know. All you can do is sit in the silence. In the dark.

I share that dream because looking back there's only one discernible thing that happened as a result of the surgeries, medications, and months on end of sheer agony: in the midst of everything, Jesus came to me.

He came to me when I was on my basement office floor. Like a prisoner of war caged in a cell, bereft of time, place, and family, I felt a presence there I had never felt before. All my Christian life I knew him but felt like I had never actually met him. At first I despised him for taking me through the valley of death just so I could meet him on the other side. But over time I learned to sit in the silence. No answers. No relief. Just him.

His presence, not his relief, was enough for me. It will be for you too.

I don't know who you are. I don't know what you're going through. I don't know what circumstances you're facing. I don't know what has ripped your heart into a thousand pieces and is throwing them back at you underhand, one tiny shard at a time, laughing.

No, not laughing, mocking.

Cancer? Loneliness? Failure? Oh yes, failure.

Whatever it is.

Hold on.

SEVEN

*INTERPERSONAL
INTERVENTION*

*I strongly suspect that if we saw all
the difference even the tiniest of our prayers make,
and all the people those little prayers were destined to affect,
and all the consequences of those prayers down through
the centuries, we would be so paralyzed with awe at
the power of prayer that we would be unable to
get up off our knees for the rest of our lives.*

PETER KREEFT, *ANGELS AND DEMONS*

ONE OF THE GREAT DEBATES in Christianity is whether
human beings make decisions by their own free will or
whether God predetermines their steps.

This chapter will no doubt be unsettling for some, because I'm going to show how God sometimes changes another person's mind when we pray for God's favor in our lives.

I mean God literally reaches down and makes someone change their mind. If your child is making destructive decisions, this will no doubt be a comforting idea. But it is unnerving when we ask, How much of what we think and do is the direct result of God favoring someone else?

When God changes a person's mind about something, I call it a Daniel 1:9 moment. Have you ever seen this happen? Let me give you an example of what I'm talking about.

In 1999 my family moved to the suburbs of Philadelphia to start a new church. We moved the day after Christmas. I told the kids they could unwrap all their Christmas gifts, but could only take one out of the box. The next day we found ourselves driving two moving trucks down the Pennsylvania Turnpike to our new home.

We didn't know a soul. It was just the five of us and our cat. (Actually, two weeks after we moved, our cat died. That's a 16.6 percent drop in attendance the second week!) There was no core group waiting for us. If this church was going to happen, we were going to have to get out and meet people.

We set our launch date for the first Sunday in October 2000, which gave us nine months to pick a church name, file tax-exempt paperwork with the government, raise additional capital for staff and equipment, recruit people to join us, and, finally, pick a place to meet on Sunday mornings.

The facilities to rent for Sunday worship services were limited. The local school district where we lived already had a tiny church meeting in the only school available, so I turned my attention to another district nearby. They told me that because of the separation of church and state they would allow basketball leagues to rent the high school, but not a church. I thought about suing the district (and was pretty sure I would have won) but thought that that might not be the best way to introduce a new church to the community.

The only option left was a brand-new movie theater complex in the area, so one morning I prayed then walked in to talk to the manager.

"Hi, my name is Brian Jones, and I'm the pastor of a new church in the area. I was wondering if I could talk to you about renting a few of your theaters on Sunday morning for church services."

"What's the name of your church?" the manager asked.

"Well, that's a *great* question! Um, we don't have a name yet."

"You don't have a name?"

"Yes. We won't open until October 1."

"I'm sorry, you want to rent space for a church that doesn't exist?" he shot back.

"Well, you see, I moved to ..." (he cut me off).

"Listen, I'm in the entertainment business, not the religion business. I can't help you."

I was crushed. I had no other options. I went to the parking lot and had two thoughts. First, for a truly irreligious person from a traditional Catholic background (which is the typical person in our area), the idea of starting a new church is just plain weird. Haven't churches existed since the beginning of time?

Later that summer we hosted a picnic at a park to get the word out about the church and recruit new people. We passed out five thousand flyers and bought a bunch of burgers, and surprisingly seventy-seven people showed up. After we had eaten I stood up to tell people about this exciting new church that was starting and then asked if they had any questions.

A lady in the back raised her hand.

"The word on the street is this new church is a cult!"

Everyone froze. Like literally their faces froze. You could feel the tension in the air. It was the first time it occurred to me that starting a new church with the last name Jones might not be a good thing (think Jim Jones, that cult leader in Guyana where everyone killed themselves when the Lord's Supper was poisoned).

I didn't know what to say. I scrambled and told them I had a master of divinity degree from Princeton Theological Seminary, that we had a sponsoring organization, and so forth. What I really wanted to say was, "Lady, I've got some special grape juice for you!" But, of course, I'd be kidding.

So my first thought after leaving the theater was—*this was going to be an uphill battle*. The second was, *I'm in trouble*.

I was completely out of options. The school wouldn't rent to me. The other district was making me pull a Judge Judy just to talk to them. There was no warehouse space to renovate. No storefronts were available. The YMCA said no. The Seventh-day Adventist Church (that meets for worship on Saturday night) thought we were weirder than the theater manager did. I was simply devastated.

After three full months of searching, I did the only thing I knew to do: I went back to the movie theater and begged.

"Like I said, I'm not in the religion business," the manager said and walked away again.

Welcome to Philly, I told myself as he shut the door behind him. (When you think of people from Philadelphia, especially *South* Philadelphia, let's just say if someone from Philly doesn't like you, you don't have to guess.)

Four months passed and still nothing.

Have you brought me half way across the country to watch me fail? I asked God.

Five months passed and I was beyond desperate.

This is what makes church planters and missionaries quit, I thought.

Finally, after six full months of searching, begging, pushing, and googling "How to sue a school district and win like in a John Grisham novel," I went to my basement and had a complete meltdown. I kicked my daughter's Barbie house, knocked over boxes, and threw books on the ground. It was pretty childish.

As I stood there panting, adrenaline coursing through my body, embarrassed for what I had just done, I felt like God was tapping me on the shoulder and saying, "Feel better now? Go back to the movie theater and ask one more time."

I screamed at the basement ceiling, "I *have been there two times!*"

"Go there one more time," I felt God impress on my heart.

I drove to the theater and sat in the parking lot for almost an hour, praying. Here was my prayer: "This is ridiculous. I'm going to look stupid. He's going to flip out on me. So God, if you want this church to happen, I need you to change the theater manager's mind. Like right now. I need you to change his mind."

I walked in and immediately saw him walking toward me in the theater lobby. I knew he was going to scream at me.

"Good morning!" he said as he saw me.

"You remember me, the church guy? Listen, I was wondering if you would be willing to reconsider letting me rent the theater on Sundays."

Before I could say another word he smiled and said, "Sure, why not?"

Wait, did he just say . . .

I was stunned.

Why not? Oh, I don't know, because I've been here twice already! I immediately thought to myself.

"Wait, you mean 'sure,' like in 'sure we can talk'? or 'sure you can . . .'" (he interrupted me again).

"I mean, sure I'll rent to you."

And he did. For six years. Until we built our own building. I couldn't believe it.

I'm convinced the hand of God literally reached down and changed his mind, for my benefit and for all those we would impact for the kingdom of God.

God literally changed his mind.

This is what I mean by a Daniel 1:9 moment.

DANIEL 1:9 MOMENTS

The book of Daniel is the story of how four young Israelite men refused to be stripped of their identities and turned into

Jason Bournes for the Babylonian military. (I'm assuming you've seen at least one of the spy thriller movies about how a young man named David Webb is changed into spy action-hero Jason Bourne.)

Because of its central location between Egypt to the southwest and the fertile lands surrounding the Tigris and Euphrates rivers to the north, Israel was constantly getting trampled by the world's superpowers.

First came the Assyrians in 721 BC, carting off northern Israel's best and brightest, and using their land as a staging area to counter Egypt.

In sixth century BC, the Assyrians were replaced by a new, emerging superpower led by an aggressive ruler named Nebuchadnezzar. Like the Assyrians before him, the Babylonians, as they were later called, set their sights once again on Egypt, if not to take them over, at least to consolidate the region against them.

Once again, Israel was caught in the middle. In 585 BC Babylonian armed forces stormed into Judah, and as a result "the Lord delivered Jehoiakim king of Judah" into Nebuchadnezzar's hands (Daniel 1:2).

The temple was plundered, the city was razed, and in a very strategic move the best and the brightest were sought out, captured, and taken back to Babylon. They were to be brainwashed and enculturated into Babylonian society as a means to strengthen the Babylonians' economy and military. Why waste people who possess leadership potential when you can strip them of their identity, transfer their loyalty, and make them work *for* you instead of *against* you?

Daniel 1:3-5 outlines the Babylonian strategy for divesting young Israelite leaders of their identities and integrating them into their military:

> Then the king ordered Ashpenaz, chief of his court officials, to bring into the king's service some of the Israelites from the royal family and the nobility—young men without any physical defect, handsome, showing aptitude for every kind of learning, well informed, quick to understand, and qualified to serve in the king's palace. He was to teach them the language and literature of the Babylonians. The king assigned them a daily amount of food and wine from the king's table. They were to be trained for three years, and after that, they were to enter the king's service.

Essentially, as the king's forces swept through the crowds, they were to hand select anyone that looked, walked, or talked like a leader. Among those chosen, four specifically are noted by the book of Daniel's author to tell their story:

> Among those who were chosen were some from Judah: Daniel, Hananiah, Mishael and Azariah. The chief official gave them new names: to Daniel, the name Belteshazzar; to Hananiah, Shadrach; to Mishael, Meshach; and to Azariah, Abednego. (Daniel 1:6-7)

The first step in taking away their identity was changing their names. Next was changing their language. The final step was changing their diet.

Israelites had very strict laws about what food they could or could not eat, and how it was to be prepared. For Daniel, food was about more than caloric intake. It was a daily test of devotion.

Not wanting to defile himself with the royal food and wine, Daniel asked the chief official overseeing his three-year acclimatization process if it would be okay if he simply ate vegetables and water (the least amount he could eat without breaking Jewish dietary laws).

Understandably the chief official refused. Eating nothing but vegetables wouldn't give his body the protein necessary to build muscle mass. He would become emaciated over time, something that would reflect very poorly on himself.

Daniel asked him to at least try letting him eat nothing but vegetables for ten days, then decide.

Let's put ourselves in the chief official's shoes. Here is a guy whose will and identity you've been charged with systematically breaking down and replacing. What possible reason would you have for allowing even the slightest hint of self-assertion and willpower to remain? There is none. To make one small allowance would jeopardize the entire effort.

Of course he wasn't going to accommodate Daniel's request. Of course he wasn't going to allow even the faintest hint of his former identity to remain. Of course he was going to say no.

But he didn't, because God intervened at that moment and changed the chief official's mind.

Daniel 1:9 says, "Now God had caused the official to show favor and compassion to Daniel."

Out of the millions of people who lived on the planet at the time, all facing their unique issues and problems, God stopped what he was doing and entered our human space-time continuum and reached down and supernaturally changed Ashpenaz's mind.

Both God and Daniel knew Ashpenaz was going to say no. Of course he was going to say no. That was his job! Then God intervened, and Ashpenaz almost robotically agreed to Daniel's experiment.

Oswald Chambers observed, "The remarkable thing about fearing God is that when you fear God, you fear nothing else, whereas if you do not fear God you fear everything else."[1]

This was certainly true in Daniel's case. The request itself was grounds for Daniel's death, but he knew this was a hill he was willing to die on.

THE DIFFERENCE BETWEEN PRAYER AND GOD'S FAVOR

Perhaps this question is on your mind right now: *What is the difference between praying and asking for God's favor?*

Isn't "praying for God's favor" just a different way of talking about prayer? Aren't they the same thing?

Yes and no. I think there is one similarity and two differences.

Both prayer and praying for favor can be single events.

Sometimes prayer and praying for God's favor refer to a single cause-and-effect event. For instance, in the Old Testament we're told that King Jehoahaz allowed God's people to follow evil practices, so the Lord allowed the King of Aram to oppress them. Seeing the error of his ways, we're told in 2 Kings 13:4-5, "Then Jehoahaz sought the LORD's favor, and the LORD listened to him, for he saw how severely the king of Aram was oppressing Israel. The LORD provided a deliverer for Israel, and they escaped from the power of Aram."

In this particular instance prayer and seeking God's favor were the same thing. Jehoahaz asks for something (the implication is he asked for deliverance) and God answers his prayer by raising up a deliverer.

But there are two other instances where prayer and seeking God's favor are clearly different.

Favor often refers to seeking help without a specific answer in mind.

More often than not, seeking God's favor refers to asking for God to do something when we don't know exactly what we need. When Jacob "begged for [God's] favor" (Hosea 12:4), we're never told what Jacob had in mind. Yes, he wanted to be rescued from his brother, but he needed more than that: reconciliation, healing, strength for him not commit suicide, and so forth. Jacob surely had a million things on his mind that he needed help with. Jacob wanted God to simply do something.

Favor often refers to a continual state of blessing.

The best way to think of favor is when we seek and find God's favor we end up being favor*ed*. We experience a continual state of receiving God's blessings without needing to stop and think about what we need and ask for them. They keep coming whether we pray or not.

I have a friend who started a new church in a unique way. He gathered a bunch of people in a room and had them call every single person that lived in a five-mile radius and invited them to their church's grand opening. They made 35,000 phone calls and 350 people showed up.

When I first heard about that, I was impressed.

"Wow, 350 people showed up because you called them on the phone?"

Then I started thinking about what it would be like to try to build a church with 350 people who *love* getting telemarketing phone calls. Can you imagine? I wondered about things like, Would they each bring their sixty-two cats to the service? Would they have any money left over to tithe after buying copious amounts of wacky insurance and timeshares and giving money to political candidates? When someone's cell phone went off in the service would they all instinctively jump up to answer it?

Believe it or not, that church has gone on to become quite an influential church in southwest Ohio. I know because Mike Mack, a good friend of mine, was one of the people who got one of their phone calls.

Mike was home one day when a woman randomly called him and asked for another person.

"I'm sorry, you have the wrong number."

"Well, how about I talk to you?" the woman said.

For the next twenty minutes, she described a new church that was starting in Centerville, Ohio. It was going to be a different kind of church, and he should come and check it out.

He did.

Soon afterward he gave his life to Christ and was baptized. Soon after that he felt called to become a pastor. Soon after that, he found himself attending a Christian college.

Today Mike is one of the leaders in our country helping churches build thriving community through small groups.

I believe that Mike's story happened because Tom, the pastor of that church, was favored, in the same way Daniel was favored. Tom didn't pray a specific prayer that God would miraculously intervene in wrong-call scenarios, any more than Daniel had prayed a specific prayer that God would intervene in his situation. God caused Mike Mack to not hang up the phone that day. God changed his mind.

God intervened in both because both Tom and Daniel were favored.

GLIMPSE INTO HEAVEN

Who do you have in your life right now whose mind needs to be changed?

Maybe it's your boss. Maybe things are rough at work right now because your boss is making bad decisions or needs to change their behavior or set a different course of action.

Maybe it's your spouse. Maybe your spouse is engaged in what author Willard Harley calls the six great "love busters" of marriage: selfish demands, disrespectful judgments, angry outbursts, dishonesty, annoying habits, and independent behavior.[2] Chances are you've tried getting them to change to no avail.

For many the greatest source of anxiety and stress is children. Regardless of age, we parents feel our hearts in our throats as we watch them face one decision after another. The situations may change over time—from not obeying in their terrible twos to making the right decisions in their twenties—but the anxiety we feel over the potential consequences of their actions remain the same.

Maybe it's a stranger. Maybe someone in a lawsuit or a business transaction, or a nameless person you're forced to rub shoulders with has the potential to make an important decision that's going to affect you negatively.

I don't know what you're facing right now, but I'm confident of one thing: God changes people minds when we're blessed by his favor.

In Revelation we're told, "When he opened the seventh seal, there was silence in heaven for about half an hour" (Revelation 8:1).

Silence in heaven for thirty minutes?

That's a strange thing to say when you think about it. Three chapters earlier in the book of Revelation, we're given a glimpse into what is going on behind the scenes in heaven. There's a nonstop interstellar worship service shaking the rafters of heaven right now.

Then I looked and heard the voice of many angels, numbering thousands upon thousands, and ten thousand times ten thousand. They encircled the throne and the living creatures and the elders. In a loud voice, they were saying:

"Worthy is the Lamb, who was slain,
to receive power and wealth and wisdom and strength
and honor and glory and praise!"

Then I heard every creature in heaven and on earth and under the earth and on the sea, and all that is in them, saying:

"To him who sits on the throne and to the Lamb
  be praise and honor and glory and power,
  for ever and ever!" (Revelation 5:11-13)

Billions of people are worshiping God, and then everything comes to a screeching halt.

Why?

The author of Revelation tells us,

And I saw the seven angels who stand before God, and seven trumpets were given to them.

Another angel, who had a golden censer, came and stood at the altar. He was given much incense to offer, with the prayers of all God's people, on the golden altar in front of the throne. The smoke of the incense, together with the prayers of the saints, went up before God from the angel's hand. (Revelation 8:2-4)

Did you catch what this is saying?

Nonstop singing is going on in heaven, and then it *stops* so the prayers of God's people on earth can reach God the Father.

This is a glimpse of what's going on in heaven right now.

Our prayers stop heaven dead in its tracks. Prayers from people like you and me. Right now. In this very instant, when you and I pray, God listens, and sometimes he chooses to answer those prayers exactly how we pray them. And sometimes that means reaching out and changing your spouse's mind because it's going to help your marriage, or changing a movie theater manager's mind because there are people who need to hear about Jesus.

The fact is when you are favor*ed* by God heaven stops to pay attention.

Sometimes God chooses *not* to answer those prayers, but sometimes he does, and whenever that happens it is but one more striking display of the unique ways God blesses his children when we ask him to bless us.

The funny thing is God is constantly bestowing his favor all around us—changing minds and hearts all around us—and all we need is the "eyes to see" and "ears to hear," as Jesus said, to notice what is happening around us.

I'll give you one last example: Computer problems are never good for anyone, but especially for someone who is a writer.

I was told by the worship pastor on my staff that when I switched over from a PC to a Mac computer, my new Mac laptop would be 100,000,000 times better than my PC because, in his exact words, "It will *never* have problems."

Macs, I was told, could withstand every attack the dark side could mount against us—cat videos on YouTube, twangy sounding country music that makes me want to jump off a bridge, and the most pernicious of all: my beloved mother's 6,234 email forwards a day ("This is funny . . . read this.").

Alas, I was sold a bill of goods. My Mac crashed this week. Twice.

To say I was ticked and frustrated is an understatement. I stormed off to my local Apple store to get it fixed.

Once in line I began rehearsing my five-point speech for the manager:

1. "Hey Mr. Apple guy, I went from PC to Mac to prevent these problems."

2. Followed by a snarky comment about how "all these unshowered hipsters standing around in blue shirts doing nothing remind me of a state highway construction crew."

3. Followed by stating that "I read Walter Isaacson's insufferably long 656-page biography about Steve Jobs, which should count for something, *anything.*"

4. Then demand a replacement for the lemon I was given.

5. End with a threat that if they don't replace this laptop on the spot, "I have 11,174 Twitter followers, and just *one tweet* to my loyal army of three real people and 11,171 bots and online get-rich-quick experts posing as real people, and we'll bring your company to a grinding halt!"

I was totally ready for 'em.

Unfortunately, Sean, the manager, never got to hear my riveting speech. I was only able to get out the words "I'm having problems" before he grabbed two techs who then patiently worked on my laptop for over an hour, ultimately fixing my problem.

I never got to express my pent-up frustration, but I did get to talk to one of the techs for over an hour about what's going on in his life and how God fits into that, and then invite him to visit our church this weekend.

Which, I realized later, was probably the reason my laptop malfunctioned in the first place. And which, when you think about it, is probably a good explanation for why we go through most of the lousy things we experience in life.

The more I talked to Sean, the more I got the sense that I was the answer to someone else's prayers.

Maybe Sean attended church as a kid and drifted away in college, never to return, and his grandma had been praying for him every day since. Maybe Sean had a falling out with his dad, and for the last three years his dad has been praying he would connect with someone who could help bridge the divide. Maybe Sean was engaged and his fiancé was praying that God would send someone into his life to be a friend or mentor. Or maybe Sean's coworker had been praying God would help open his eyes to spiritual realities.

I had no clue who, or what, precipitated our meeting, but of one thing I am certain: someone had prayed into existence a Daniel 1:9 moment for Sean, and I had walked right into it.

EIGHT

REDEMPTIVE POVERTY

*To be clever enough to get a great deal of money,
one must be stupid enough to want it.*

G. K. Chesterton, *A Miscellany of Men*

'M STANDING NAKED BEFORE A ROOM full of strangers and I know that I should never run. Running only makes things worse.

So, I count to ten and wait for a few small animals to cross my path. The most common ones to appear are beagles, baby llamas, and Persian cats. I don't know why that is. It just is. Anyway, I pick two of them up, cover myself, and then slowly walk off stage left.

I know that if I run, they will chase me. And being chased will only lead me to run aimlessly through crowded city streets, usually in New York City. When that happens, it gets progressively worse. I start bumping into old teachers from grade school, my dentist, and the grocery store checkout clerk. My heart starts racing. My palms get sweaty. Sweat pours down my face, and as soon as that happens the zombies start walking out of abandoned buildings.

Between randomly running up 7th Avenue in Manhattan, impaling zombies while my deceased eighty-six-year-old grandmother is running alongside me asking if I have her old peanut butter fudge recipe (which I lost), it dawns on me that no matter how hard I try, I just can't get home.

Each turn leads to another turn, and another, and another, until at long last I turn a corner and find myself at a dead-end, unable to turn around. The zombies, my pastor, and my fourth-grade teacher, Mrs. Johnson, *all* close in on me. I realize I shouldn't have run, but by now it's too late.

So this is how it ends, I think to myself.

I throw a llama at the zombies because by now I don't care that I'm naked, I just want to get out alive. With their arms terrifyingly outstretched, pressing, closing in, I scream, but the words won't come out.

It's like someone is choking me.

I move side to side, trying to call for help.

I kick. I punch. I feel a shove on my shoulder.

This is it.

Then another push.

I'm going to die!

Then someone hits me in my thigh.

No! This is it! God help me!

Then a painful jab to my side.

Screams muffled. Heart racing. Everyone and everything is pressing in on me!

Then one final zombie hits me, right in the ribs, and I slowly open my eyes.

I hear my wife say, "Hey, roll over! You're snoring!"

I've been sleeping this whole time.

That, my friends, is what it feels like to have an anxiety dream.

TSUNAMI OF FINANCIAL BLESSINGS

They say that what we suppress during the day we dream about at night.

I'm pretty sure I don't suppress the imminent threat of a zombie apocalypse. What I fear is something much scarier.

People who study dreams say we take the abstract feelings of what we carry during the day, and then create concrete images and scenarios in our dreams to help us process what we can't, or won't, process while we're awake.

That's why what we're *feeling* in our dreams is a pretty good indicator of how we're feeling in real life. If we're anxious and disquieted in our dreams, there's a good chance that's how we're feeling, even if we don't appear to be anxious while we're awake.

For example, in my book *Getting Rid of the Gorilla*, I tell the story about how my wife, Lisa, and I went to a neighborhood pizza shop for a special occasion.[1]

For the first two years of our marriage, Lisa and I were broke. We were both finishing school full-time, and the small amount of income I generated came from building computers during the week and preaching at a small rural church on the weekends.

One night we decided to get a slice of pizza.

We were in a hurry and barely had enough money to buy a small pizza. Next to us sat a table full of police officers eating a culinary feast—pizza, salads, and dessert.

When they got up, they left four pieces of pizza on their table, and I looked at Lisa and asked, "Are you thinking what I'm thinking?" She answered, "Absolutely not!" To try to soothe her conscience, I gave her a passionate speech about not wasting God's resources and how God would be happy if we ate that pizza. She didn't buy it.

When the coast was clear, I gingerly slid the pizza onto our table, and we shoved the pieces into our mouths. Seconds later Lisa looked up and yelled, "Sheez!" Two police officers were coming back to the table next to us, and one had a to-go box in his hands! With an entire piece of pizza in my mouth, I stared at Lisa and said in a muffled voice, "Game faces, woman. Hold it together. Breathe. Don't crack! I'm not going to the big house over this."

No doubt you have a story or two of a period in your life when you struggled financially. Maybe you're struggling right now. I remember those times not so much by what we couldn't afford but by how I felt when I woke up in the morning—anxious, always fearful, feeling my back was constantly up against the wall. The odd thing is I don't remember feeling that way during the day.

What I suppressed during the day (anxiety) worked itself out in my dreams at night (crazy running from zombies dreams).

I'll never forget a specific event that gave me a tremendous sense of hope that things would change financially.

I heard on a local Christian radio station that a famous TV evangelist was coming to a local church in the area. I had seen him a couple of times on TV and was impressed, so I dragged Lisa out on a Wednesday night to hear him.

That night he talked about God's favor, the exact topic of this book, and how if we trusted in Christ and asked for God's blessings on our finances, that God would shock us by the ways he would supernaturally meet our needs.

"Come forward and make a seed gift," he told everyone there. As that country song goes, beware of the preacher who asks you to give God your money but gives you his address.

We had exactly $120 in our checking account. I wrote a check for $80, figuring that we'd need $40 to get us by until Friday when the tsunami of financial blessings started to roll in. Gauging by the hundreds of people that went up to the front with me, I figured there were some pretty hurting people there that night.

I know this is going to come as quite a shock, but the Brinks truck didn't show up at our apartment complex on Friday. Nor the next week. Nor any time soon.

I had to ask for a ten-day extension on the rent and was forced to put $30 worth of groceries on the credit card. As expected, the zombies came after me in my dreams that weekend, the TV evangelist kept traveling the country bilking financially destitute people out of their money, and I became one jaded candidate for the ministry.

I remember asking God for his favor on our finances as vividly today as when I first uttered the words.

Instead of things getting better, they got much worse. For the next two and a half years, Lisa and I ate generic fish sticks,

Kool-Aid without the sugar mixed in, and anything else we could buy in the generic aisle for $20 a week.

I can still hear her cousin's words, who, while visiting us, opened the refrigerator door and saw only a tub of generic butter: "Geez! Are you guys poor or something?"

Why hadn't God answered my prayer and financially blessed us with his favor? I was 110 percent committed to my faith. I was willing to surrender anything, go anywhere, and do anything I was asked. Why did things get worse?

ABOUNDING WITH FAVOR

One of the questions I like to ask people when I'm trying to make small talk is, "If you could go back in time and see any event happen in the Bible, what would you choose to see?"

What would be your top choices?

I think seeing the waters divide during the exodus would be pretty amazing. No doubt, watching Elijah's showdown with the prophets of Baal on Mt. Carmel would be something to behold. For me, however, I would have liked to have been there for Moses' final address to God's people in Deuteronomy 33, right before he died.

When I was younger, I was undoubtedly more impressed by the action stories, miracles, and displays of power in Scripture. But as I've grown older I've grown more impressed by kindness, people who persevere, and tracing the long-term impact of people's lives on other people.

I would have loved to talk to Moses after a lifetime of spiritual leadership. I would have loved peppering him with questions about how to come back from failure, leading

God's people in change, and what it was like to walk on holy ground.

But I would loved to have seen him on the day he was helped to his feet to address God's people as they stood on the edge of the Promised Land.

After recounting how the Lord's hand brought them to that point, Moses began going down the list of the twelve tribes of Israel and giving each tribe a specific blessing.

To the thousands there that day that belonged to the tribe of Benjamin, he blessed them by saying,

> Let the beloved of the LORD rest secure in him,
>> for he shields him all day long,
>> and the one the LORD loves rests between his shoulders.
> (Deuteronomy 33:12)

To those in the tribe of Zebulun he said,

> Rejoice, Zebulun, in your going out,
>> and you, Issachar, in your tents.
> They will summon peoples to the mountain
>> and there offer the sacrifices of the righteous;
> they will feast on the abundance of the seas,
>> on the treasures hidden in the sand. (Deuteronomy 33:18-19)

Each tribe, descended from and named after a son of Jacob, was given a specific blessing.

I point this out because when Moses comes to the tribe of Naphtali, he gave them a specific blessing of God's favor that was both financial and tied to the location they were to inhabit once Joshua led them into the Promised Land.

> Naphtali is abounding with the favor of the LORD
> > and is full of his blessing;
> > he will inherit southward to the lake.
> > (Deuteronomy 33:23)

Naphtali would be a tribe "abounding with God's favor." The implication, of course, is that this meant God would bless them with financial and material blessings.

I believe this happens. I believe there are times when we pray for God's favor, and he responds with financial blessings. This happens to be one of those occasions.

What I'd like for you to note is the location where Moses said the tribe of Naphtali was to settle once they ventured into the land of Israel.

They were to settle in the land "southward to the lake."

To what lake is he referring and where is that, exactly?

The body of water Moses was talking about was called Lake Gennesaret, or what is translated in our New Testament Bible as the Sea of Galilee.

Sound familiar?

Yes, Moses said that the tribe of Naphtali would settle in the exact area that more than a thousand years later would become the hometown area of Jesus.

BLESSED POOR?

Historians tell us that the area surrounding Lake Gennesaret was an agricultural Garden of Eden. No wonder Moses said that Naphtali would "abound in the favor of the LORD." Out of all the tribes, Naphtali hit the jackpot.

The Roman historian Josephus called the area an "earthly paradise."[2] Look at how he described the land Naphtali was about to inhabit:

> The country also that lies over against this lake hath the same name of Gennesareth; its nature is wonderful as well as its beauty; its soil is so fruitful that all sorts of trees can grow upon it, and the inhabitants accordingly plant all sorts of trees there; for the temper of the air is so well mixed, that it agrees very well with those several sorts, particularly walnuts, which require the coldest air, flourish there in vast plenty; there are palm trees also, which grow best in hot air; fig trees also and olives grow near them, which yet require an air that is more temperate.
>
> One may call this place the ambition of nature, where it forces those plants that are naturally enemies to one another to agree together; it is a happy contention of the seasons, as if every one of them laid claim to this country; for it not only nourishes different sorts of autumnal fruit beyond men's expectation, but preserves them a great while.[3]

If you had to pick a pre–Industrial Revolution area to live, this was the place. By all indications, there would *never* come a day when people living around the Lake of Gennesaret would lack anything.

A thousand years later Jesus launched a teaching ministry in and around the shores of the same lake. "One day as Jesus was standing by the Lake of Gennesaret, the people were crowding around him and listening to the word of God" (Luke 5:1). Think about that. Over a thousand years later, in the same area first settled by the tribe of Naphtali, Jesus performed most of his miracles and delivered the majority of his teachings.

One such lesson is called either the Sermon on the Mount (found in Matthew 5–8) or the Sermon on the Plain (found in Luke 6). Much of the material found in Luke 6 is also in Matthew 5–8. Since Jesus no doubt taught the same material at different times and adapted it for different audiences, we would expect similar but different discourses like these two.

Luke's version of this sermon begins,

> He went down with them and stood on a level place. A large crowd of his disciples was there and a great number of people from all over Judea, from Jerusalem, and from the coastal region around Tyre and Sidon, who had come to hear him and to be healed of their diseases. Those troubled by impure spirits were cured, and the people all tried to touch him, because power was coming from him and healing them all. (Luke 6:17-19)

This large crowd of people came from the same towns and villages first established on land allotted by Moses and gifted to the tribe of Naphtali. These were descendants of people who told they would be "abounding in the favor of the LORD."

Jesus' audience was living, as Josephus put it, in "the ambition of nature."

Yet, what were the first words out of Jesus' mouth?

Looking at his disciples, he said:
> "Blessed are you who are poor,
>   for yours is the kingdom of God.

Blessed are you who hunger now,
for you will be satisfied." (Luke 6:20-21)

Did you catch that?

Often the Hebrew concept of *favor* can be translated "blessed" or "blessing" in the New Testament. This was one such occasion.

Like Moses' audience, Jesus' audience too was "abounding in favor." They were "blessed."

But unlike Moses, Jesus told his hearers they were blessed not because they would become wealthy but because they were poor. These people were blessed *because* they were poor. They were blessed *because* they were hungry. Poverty was a sign of God's blessing.

Now you might be familiar with Matthew's version that reads, "Blessed are the poor *in spirit*." Matthew 5:3 records Jesus words as not necessarily being about poverty itself but about being emotionally destitute.

Which is correct?

Both.

Jesus, no doubt, taught both variations of this teaching on different occasions.

I highlight this because I want you to see the stark relief between the "abounding in favor" comment that was shared by Moses and the poverty that Jesus' audience no doubt faced over a thousand years later.

BEYOND CONSUMPTION

When we pray for God's favor, one of the ways he responds is by providing for our financial needs, much like we talked about in chapter five.

However, we must acknowledge that just as often God responds to our cries for blessing by making us poorer. That's right; poverty can be a sign of God's favor just as much as wealth.

As Americans living in a twenty-first-century, consumer-driven capitalistic culture, it is hard for us to imagine how being forced to live with less could be a sign of God's favor, but there are two truths I want you to consider.

The more we consume, the more in bondage we are. On his website, BecomingMinimalist.com, author Joshua Becker notes,

~ There are 300,000 items in the average American home (*LA Times*).

~ The average size of the American home has nearly tripled in size over the past 50 years (NPR).

~ And still, 1 out of every 10 Americans rent offsite storage —the fastest growing segment of the commercial real estate industry over the past four decades (*New York Times Magazine*).

~ Shopping malls outnumber high schools. And 93% of teenage girls rank shopping as their favorite pastime (*Affluenza*).[4]

We have to ask ourselves, *is this normal?*

The answer is obviously *no.*

Forget what the Bible says. Forget God, Jesus, truth, heaven, hell, and dozens of other theological concepts. All we have to do is travel to another country—virtually any country—to discover that something is wrong with the typical American lifestyle.

My dad was born in a one-room house on the bank of the Mud Creek in Harold, Kentucky. He never saw more than the bare minimum of food set out for dinner until his grand-father's funeral when he was ten.

My wife's aunt often reminds us that when she was a child she routinely received an orange for Christmas. She didn't know she was poor. She thought that was normal. Nobody at the time received extravagant gifts like we give today.

Most families are one or two generations from stories like this. For the vast majority of people on the planet, this is normal living, today.

Most people in India don't shop as a form of entertainment; they shop to survive.

To find out how tied we are to our possessions, we would do well to follow the advice of the great Roman Stoic phi-losopher Seneca.

Seneca, a contemporary of Jesus, wrote a series of letters to his friend Lucillius, giving him advice from the perspective of Stoic philosophy on how to train his mind to be freed from the worry of poverty.

In letter 18 of Seneca's *Moral Letters to Lucillius*, while talking about taking risks in business and life, he challenges his friend:

> Set aside a certain number of days, during which you shall be content with the scantiest and cheapest fare, with coarse and rough dress, saying to yourself the while: *"Is this the condition that I feared?"*
>
>   It is precisely in times of immunity from care that the soul should toughen itself beforehand for occasions of greater stress.[5]

In other words, make it a regular practice to pick a few days periodically to eat rice and beans, wear a ragged T-shirt and jeans, and don't shave or shower. Walk around like that for a weekend every month or so, and while doing so ask yourself, "Is this the condition that I feared?"

Why do that? To toughen the soul for times of greater stress. To quiet our souls from having anxiety-ridden zombie dreams. To gain perspective. To feel freedom. To separate our perception of blessing from the consumption of material possessions.

The less we own, the more freedom we have. Not only do we consume resources and discard waste exponentially faster than the rest of the world's population, but having all this stuff doesn't give us freedom; it steals it from us.

Recently a Facebook friend lost his job and had to downsize virtually everything in his life. He posted, "Just turned 49 and moved into my mom's basement—THIS. IS. THE. LIFE."

We're the same age, and while it must have been a terribly emotional experience to lose his job like that, it got me thinking.

I'm fifty, married, and have three kids (two are in college) and a mortgage. I feel like I'm a handyman, financial planner, professional shopper, and full-time worrier all rolled into one. Unlike my friend who lost everything, I manage the upkeep on five used cars for my family members, a home that needs constant maintenance, paying bills on things like electricity, taxes, sewage, and life insurance, and a list of other responsibilities that could take another two to three paragraphs.

And I wonder if all of those responsibilities keep me from feeling free.

Now, of course, these are things I've chosen to take on and wouldn't change. My family and I need a place to live. We need to pay the sewage bill. We like to eat. Having life insurance is a good thing.

But if we were forced to live with no cars (and had to walk to work or take public transportation) and didn't have to pay a mortgage (and were forced instead to rent a much smaller and cheaper place), under what definition could I realistically consider that tragic? For the majority of people alive on this planet, this is life.

But more important, this can also be freedom.

Despite all my anxiety dreams, I remember what it was like to be married and completely broke, and I *long* to feel that way again.

We weren't tied to anything.

The future was wide open.

We could have moved to California to go to graduate school, or we could have just as easily moved to Burkina Faso to be missionaries.

Possessions didn't possess us. We were totally free.

The rabbis during Jesus' time used a derogatory phrase to describe the people Jesus was talking to in his Sermon on the Plain. They called them the "people of the land."

They were the dirty people—the migrant laborers who were paid pennies on the dollar to break their backs picking fruit on the expansive farms surrounding Lake of Gennesaret. They were uneducated, simple people, the kind sometimes characterized as lazy, government-money bilking leeches.

What Jesus fought so hard to get them to understand—to get us to understand—is that the fewer possessions we have, the more blessed we are.

It's easier, Jesus said, for rich people to shimmy their way through a hole in a needle than it is for them to squeeze their way into living under God's rule.

We cannot serve both God and money, he said. Anxiety comes when we try.

December 2016 I went to Africa to investigate how our church could partner with missionaries in an area surrounding Lake Turkana in northwest Kenya. The Turkana people, as they're called by anthropologists, live a notch above cavemen in little huts built on the mud. I'm talking *National Geographic* kind of stuff.

As we were waiting in the Lodwar (Kenya) airport (which was nothing more than a small building next to an airstrip made of gravel) to catch a plane back to Nairobi, I happened to be sitting next to a missionary who worked in a remote area an hour north.

She was my age. Single. Graduated with a master's degree. She struck me as the kind of person so talented you would be reading her books instead of mine or would be attending a church she served if she remained behind in the United States. As a young woman, she decided she wanted to be a missionary, so as a single woman in her early twenties she moved to Africa to serve some of the most unreached people left on the planet at the time.

She has spent her entire adult life working in Turkana as a missionary doing leadership training and church planting. She lives in a place smaller than the shed in your backyard. For fun she gathers with other missionaries once a month, a few hours away, and celebrates birthdays and anniversaries.

She has no car.

She doesn't have junk that she doesn't need stored somewhere in a basement.

She doesn't care about clothing trends, stock options, or what restaurant to go to after church.

And she has joy.

And time.

Yes, time. Remember what that was? Time to build real relationships. To laugh. To pursue hobbies that excite her. To sleep.

She has the kind of life that people work their whole careers to save up enough money to get once they retire.

But she has that life.

Right now.

NINE

DIVINE CONFIRMATION

*My Lord God, I have no idea where I am going. I do not see
the road ahead of me. I cannot know for certain where it will end.
Nor do I really know myself, and the fact that I think
that I am following your will does not mean
that I am actually doing so.*

THOMAS MERTON, *THOUGHTS IN SOLITUDE*

ONE OF THE THINGS WE CHRISTIANS struggle with is
trying to discern whether God is calling us to do something.
If you're not a person of faith and somehow picked up this book,
this statement might strike you as odd. The idea of God alone
seems over the top for many, never mind adding the notion that

among the billions of people on the planet this God might try to guide your thoughts and actions.

Yet, that's what we believe, but let me share a few caveats about this before we go further (lest you really think we're crazy).

CAVEAT 1: GOD RARELY SPEAKS IN AN AUDIBLE VOICE ANYMORE

Years ago I used to frequent another church's Saturday night service. I was pretty burned out at the time, and I really liked the pastor of the church, so I'd sneak over there every once in a while to get a spiritual shot in the arm.

I'll never forget one Saturday night the worship pastor telling the congregation,

> In my prayer time this week God told me that we are supposed to begin taking our worship to the streets. So what we're going to do is rent a huge flatbed truck, put our entire worship team on it, hook our speakers up to a generator and drive it through the streets playing worship music and lifting our hands to Jesus!

That's just wonderful, I thought, *because people don't already think Christians are freaky enough.*

The problem, in my mind, wasn't the goal. As stupid as I thought the idea was at the time, I appreciated their desire to "get out in the streets." And the problem wasn't the method. While I'm not sure turning ten artsy people loose on a flatbed truck with microphones and speakers was the safest thing to do without Apache helicopter air support, at least they were trying something to reach their family and friends for Jesus.

The problem was the phrase "God told me."

Whenever someone tells you something that begins with the three words *God told me* (and they mean in an audible voice) you should immediately

~ Look for the nearest exit.

~ If said exit is locked, attempt to cut them off mid-sentence by poking them in the eye.

~ If they are significantly taller than you and hence out of eye-poking reach, quickly lift your pant legs as high as possible because you are about to wade through a pile of really smelly stuff.

Let me be clear: God has never spoken directly to me, ever.

~ Not through a dream.

~ Not through a strange set of circumstances.

~ Not through a person.

~ Not in my head.

~ Not in my spirit.

~ Not in my gut.

~ Not one time. Never. Nada. Zip.

In all my years walking on this planet, I can say with the utmost confidence that the Creator of the heavens and the earth has *never* spoken directly to me.

But ...

There have been numerous times that I've felt confident that God has spoken to me *indirectly*.

~ Through a dream.

~ Through a strange set of circumstances.

~ Through people.

~ In my head.

~ In my spirit.

~ In my gut.

The problem is when those times occurred, I wasn't sure if it was God that was communicating with me, or if I had too much pizza the night before.

And that's the issue—we're never completely sure, are we? As convinced as we are that we're hearing from God, the only time we should ever feel 100 percent certain God is *speaking directly to us* is when we are reading the Bible.

All other times lack that certainty,

~ regardless of how good the moment feels,

~ or if you have a mountaintop experience at a church camp bonfire,

~ or if a trusted pastor is sharing some startling revelation about your future,

~ or especially when everything within your soul screams that what you are sensing is coming directly from the throne room of God.

In all of these times, take whatever information, prompting, or leading you think is coming directly from God with a graceful measure of incredulity.

Jeremiah 17:9 says,

> The heart is deceitful above all things
>> and beyond cure.
>> Who can understand it?

The annals of church history are filled with stories of people who thought they heard from God but sadly didn't. This is true of me.

CAVEAT 2: DISCERNING WHAT GOD IS CALLING YOU TO DO IS NOT A SUPERMYSTICAL PROCESS

Not only should Christians stop using the phrase "God told me," they should find another synonym for the word *called*.

That word has caused more guilt, frustration, and confusion than any other word in the Christian vocabulary.

I hear Christians ask all the time,

~ How do I know if I am being *called* to take or leave this job?

~ Was I *called* to serve in this ministry area?

~ How do I know if God is *calling* me to do _____?

~ I'm scared God will *call* me to become a missionary. Will he do that?

~ Is God *calling* me into the ministry?

I wish the word never existed. It simply confuses what should be a very simple process for discerning God's will:

Calling = Desire + Gifting + Opportunity

That's it.

If you want to do something (desire) but don't have the skills to pull it off (gifts) or the chance to make that happen (opportunity), you're not *called*.

If you have the innate talent or ability (gifts) to do something, but don't want to do it (desire) and the door hasn't opened for that to happen (opportunity), you're not *called*.

If you have the chance to do something (opportunity) but don't have a lick of talent in you to pull it off (gifts) and wouldn't want to do it even if you were paid a gazillion dollars (desire), you're not *called*.

If you want to do something, people have told you that you are pretty good at it, and are given a chance (or you can make it happen in an entrepreneurial sense), then you have been *called*.

Congratulations.

But someone might ask, how do I know when I am *uncalled*?

It's very simple.

Take one of those three factors away.

21 WORDS THAT WILL CHANGE YOUR LIFE

Eliminating the clichés of "God told me" and "called" from our vocabulary clears the way for having a frank discussion about another way God shows us his favor when we ask for it: by giving us unmistakable confirmation that he's at work leading, guiding, and calling us to do something.

I know that sounds 110 percent in direct contradiction from the two caveats I just shared, but it's not.

Hang with me.

The name Gideon is near synonymous with the idea of discerning God's will. Undoubtedly you've heard of people "putting out a fleece."

The idea comes from the story in Judges 6, where the Israelite leader Gideon tried to discern whether God was leading him to mount a military attack on the Midianites, a local tribe that was oppressing Israel.

Leading people into battle has a tendency to, well, to get you killed, so we can understand why Gideon was a tad reluctant to head off without a high measure of certainty that God was directing him. To ensure he wasn't crazy and hearing things, he proposed a simple solution: Gideon told God he would place a piece of wool on the ground overnight, and if in the morning after the dew had fallen the wool itself was drenched, but the ground around it was dry, he would know that God was leading him to mount an attack. Not too shabby of a proposal.

Hence the common Christian phrase *setting out a fleece* in an attempt to discern God's will for a situation.

As you would expect, in the morning the fleece was so drenched that when Gideon squeezed it there was enough water to fill a large bowl.

That's pretty conclusive divine confirmation.

I share that story not because of the fleece but because of the verses that immediately precede the fleece incident, which provide a larger perspective on how Gideon approached discerning the will of God.

After years of Midianite raids on the cities of Israel, we're told,

The angel of the LORD came and sat down under the oak in Ophrah that belonged to Joash the Abiezrite, where his son Gideon was threshing wheat in a winepress to keep it from the Midianites. When the angel of the LORD appeared to Gideon, he said, "The LORD is with you, mighty warrior." (Judges 6:11-12)

First, I have to pause and say, Best. Nickname. Ever.

Who wouldn't love to know that when God and the angels looked at you, they called you "mighty warrior"? What do you think your heavenly nickname is? You know we probably all have one, right? Mine would is probably, "The Lord is with you, he who watches too much college football."

Gideon had obviously distinguished himself as a leader of men, a warrior *par excellence*. He was the go-to guy to lead an insurgency, but before he laid his life on the line in what had to be a near suicide mission, he had to be convinced he wasn't crazy.

Let's admit to ourselves something we Christians lose sight of, but which Gideon had a clear handle on: it's foolish to think there is a God out there who wants to guide our thoughts and behavior. At least from the perspective of nonbelievers.

The potential for self-deception—convincing ourselves that we're hearing, seeing, or sensing something from God—is so high that having a person like Gideon as a mentor is helpful.

"Pardon me, my lord," Gideon replied, "but if the LORD is with us, why has all this happened to us? Where are all his wonders that our ancestors told us about when they said, 'Did not the LORD bring us up out of Egypt?' But now the LORD has abandoned us and given us into the hand of Midian." (v. 13)

Great question! I love this Gideon guy. He gets to the heart of the matter in seconds. If God cared so much, why was he letting these things happen in the first place?

What was the answer? The Lord turned to him and said, "Go in the strength you have and save Israel out of Midian's hand. Am I not sending you?" (v. 14). In other words, the answer to the question "why does God allow us to suffer" is the same answer every person in the Bible is given: (1) I'm not telling you why, and (2) I am sending you to solve the problem.

Gideon, a man who has one foot firmly planted in faith and the other in what he can observe with his own eyes, asks the obvious follow-up question, "Pardon me, my lord . . . but how can I save Israel? My clan is the weakest in Manasseh, and I am the least in my family" (v. 15).

I love this guy. "Uh hum, pardon me . . ."

They were small. They were weak. Gideon was puny. It was obvious to anyone that had eyes to see.

Gideon didn't realize that with God, the battle is never determined by what *we* can see but what God sees within us.

Not tall enough? Not educated enough? Not from the "right" family? Doesn't matter. Can you trust? That's all that the Lord requires. "The LORD answered, 'I will be with you, and you will strike down all the Midianites, leaving none alive'" (v. 16).

Then, in what has to be one of the most important lessons ever recorded in the Bible for future generations to read, Gideon uttered the twenty-one most important words anyone could ask when trying to discern the will of God on an issue: "If now I have found favor in your eyes, give me a sign that it is really you talking to me" (v. 17).

There's our word again.

One of the greatest barriers to experiencing God's presence and power in our lives is overanalyzing things. Our brains, as useful as they are, can become a barrier to following Jesus at times.

Have you ever noticed that the one thing that sets bold and faithful followers of Jesus apart from timid and unfaithful ones is their simple obedience?

He said, "Follow me," and they did.

He said, "Do this," and they tried.

He said, "Try this," and they gave it their best shot.

Following Jesus hasn't changed. Jesus comes to us today and says, "follow me" or "do this" or "try this," and how do we respond?

Is that Jesus talking to me? we ask.

What if I'm misunderstanding what he wants me to do? we wonder.

So how do we respond? We stall. We read the Bible some more. We get a second and third opinion. We stall some more. We pray some more.

On and on it goes.

Can you imagine what would have happened if Peter had responded to Jesus the way we do when he asked him to walk to him on the water? Can you imagine how the story would have been different if Peter's response was, "Can I first consult my prayer partner?"

LORD, GIVE ME A SIGN

I want to encourage you to let the story of Gideon take on a much more central role in your life.

"If now I have found favor in your eyes, give me a sign that it is really you talking to me" is not just a great storyline from an dusty old book from the annals of history; it is a key operational guideline for finding, obeying, and staying in the will of God.

When we ask God for his favor, he provides startling clarity around decisions when we're trying to discern his will.

Sometimes when we ask for God's favor, he responds by giving us a specific, tangible sign of divine confirmation that allows us to take our next step with confidence.

The situation in Honduras was a perfect example.

I went to Honduras to discern whether this was a country and a region where God wanted us to plant churches. His response? My entire family almost got whacked by thugs in the middle of a coup.

That was a pretty clear sign.

Now I think there are a few suggestions about how to ask for a sign from the Lord.

Look to Scripture first. Everything you want to know about what God thinks about life, loving, and living is contained in the Bible. I've found that almost every situation I've faced in life when I needed direction, the guidance I needed was already provided in a principle in Scripture.

We should only ask for a sign after exhaustively examining Scripture for the guidance we need, if for no other reason than I doubt God will give someone a sign when one has already been provided in his Word.

Don't ask for a sign as a way to sidestep patience and suffering. You might be tempted to ask God to give you a sign when all you're doing is trying to force God's hand in a matter. You can't sidestep the wisdom-building process of trials and tribulations God takes all of us through.

Ask for a sign only when you're forced to do so. If you must make a decision and can't wait, and there's nothing written about it in Scripture, and you can't decide which direction God would have you go, then ask for a sign.

Wait until you have an A or B scenario. You can't ask for a sign when you have sixteen options to choose from. Wait to ask God for a sign when you have used your godly wisdom, trusted advice, and searched the Scripture to narrow your choices down to only two—an A choice and a B choice.

Don't get all televangelisty. If trying to decide what job to take, or whether to make a significant purchase, and the decision is weighing on you, don't ask God to cause an earthquake somewhere or to allow you to levitate in the air tomorrow when you wake up. Make it simple, normal, doable, and, for all that is holy and pure, don't ask God to "speak to you." You're asking for a sign, not a voice.

Ask for an abnormal occurrence of an everyday occurrence. After everything I've read in church history and spiritual biographies, after talking to friends, and through what I've learned from my own life, I've found that God works best when you give him realistic, everyday options.

Here's an example of what not to do:

I'll never forget the time soon after becoming a Christian when I was trying to discern where God wanted me to serve as a missionary.

"Okay God," I remember praying. "I'm going to lean back, close my eyes, and the first country that pops into my head—I promise you that I will move there and spend the rest of my life trying to reach those people."

With all the impulsive recklessness a newly converted eighteen-year-old with the gift of evangelism could muster, I leaned back, cleared my mind, and waited.

Seconds later the word *Greenland* came to mind.

"Okay, let's try this again," I thought.

Here's a better example: Around the same time I was trying to discern whether God wanted me to be a missionary to somewhere else in the world or in the United States (i.e., church planter), friends of mine were going through the same process.

They were trying to decide whether God wanted them to (1) serve a church in Kentucky that had invited the husband to be their senior minister, or (2) prepare to go to Venezuela to be missionaries.

Their decision fit all the right criteria. Both were encouraged in Scripture. They had two choices, not fifty-six. They wanted to do both. They were encouraged to do both by family and friends. They simply couldn't decide.

So they set out a fleece.

Before they went to bed that night, they prayed together as a couple and said, "God, if you want us to go to Venezuela, please wake us up at exactly 2 a.m. in the morning."

Sounds kinda crazy, huh?

They went to sleep that night, knowing that since they were both sound sleepers, if God truly wanted them to serve in Caracas, they would need a realistic, doable sign that didn't jeopardize millions of lives in a tsunami affecting a majority world country somewhere.

They went to sleep like they normally did.

Same bedtime.

Same routine.

Yet on this night, something mysterious happened.

He woke up in the middle of the night, sat straight up in bed, looked over at the clock, and there it was staring at him in red numbers: 2 a.m.

He shook his wife.

She leaned over and saw it, and the two of them spent over two decades serving in one of the most fruitful mission efforts I have ever observed.

TEN

STRATEGIC FAILURE

We think in terms of apostolic journeys.
God dares to put His greatest ambassadors in chains.

Watchman Nee, *The Normal Christian Life*

ONE OF THE REASONS WE SEEK GOD'S FAVOR on our lives is so that we can be successful.

But *success* can be hard to define. Let's talk about a few examples of what it's not so we can more clearly see what it is.

You're not successful if you destroy your health along the way.

This should be a no-brainer for most, but it's not.

Occasionally other pastors ask me to coach them on how to more effectively serve the people God has called them to reach. I don't have the time to do this as often as I'd like, but when I get a chance, it is a real honor. First, I ask them to do four things: (1) get a complete physical, (2) hire a personal trainer, (3) see a dietician, and (4) completely redesign their bedroom for optimal sleep.

Once these things are set in motion, I help them identify their priorities that will have the greatest effect in their ministry. Then I have them show me which hours during the day they will act on these priorities. I do not exaggerate when I say that 100 percent of the time they'll have five or six activities they'll *say* are essential, but for which there is no time left to accomplish them. I guarantee we'd find the same thing if I sat down with you. That's because if God is calling you to do something great, you'll always come up with more things to do than time allows. We become our own worst enemies.

God expects you to work hard, but he does not want you to become a workaholic. Remember, in God's eyes people are worth dying for, success is not. Never confuse the two. As Henry Blackaby wrote in *Spiritual Leadership*,

> God has a plan for each person that is uniquely suited to that individual. Unlike people, God never piles on more than someone can handle. God never overbooks people. God never drives his servants to the point of breakdown. God never burns people out. God never gives people tasks that are beyond the strength or ability he provides.[1]

You're not successful if you destroy your family along the way.

One of my favorite leadership books is Warren Bennis and Patricia Ward Biederman's *Organizing Genius: The Secrets of*

Creative Collaboration. I found their stories of what great groups of focused people can accomplish incredibly inspiring. I loved everything about the book except one single line: "Great Groups are full of indefatigable people who are struggling to turn a vision into a machine and whose lawns and goldfish have died of neglect. Such people don't stay up nights wondering if they are spending enough time with the children."[2]

Listen, if you're being honored for doing great work, but you've lost your family in the process, you've lost, period. God knows that once you desire to do something well, you'll have to decide where you're going to cut back. You can't do everything. You have only so much time. God totally gets that. When *God* calls you to do something, your family is always a *part* of that vision, not separate from it. It's not either-or. If somehow you've convinced yourself that is not the case, you're operating off the wrong definition of success.

But I'm not judging you at all. Trying to hit it out of the park with every area of your life is hard. I know.

So often I feel like a circus clown who tries to keep ten plates spinning at the same time. Watching someone go back and forth frantically trying to keep all their plates spinning in life is entertaining, as long as it isn't you.

When my kids were younger, the biggest stress as a parent wasn't deciding where to eat after church, but making sure we had all the kids in the car when we got to the restaurant. As my kids grew, trying to keep the plates spinning—loving my wife, raising our daughters, staying in shape, doing my best at work, staying connected to my parents and siblings, managing our money, caring for the house, sharing my faith, deepening friendships, and getting our kids to soccer practice with both shin guards—was next to impossible. Surprisingly, the problem has not changed the older I've gotten. Responsibilities shift, but pressures do not.

The thing that most distresses me about not being able to keep up with all the competing demands in life is that I know deep down this isn't a time-management issue, it is a power issue. I can't keep up because I literally *cannot* keep up. I don't have it in me. Even if there were ten of me standing before the ten most important plates in my life, I still couldn't be the person I need to be for each of those situations. I am exhausted, not because of a lack of physical energy or time constraints, but because everything I have been, am, and will be is still not enough to keep all my plates in the air.

Barbara Brown Taylor summed up my predicament when she wrote, "I do not mean to make an idol of health, but it does seem to me that at least some of us have made an idol of exhaustion. The only time we know we have done enough is when we are running on empty and when the ones we love most are the ones we see the least."[3]

SUCCESS REDEFINED

Here's a new definition of *success* I want you to begin using: *success is finding favor with God.*

That's true success.

If we have God's stamp of approval on our lives—meaning, if we're doing the things he has called us to do—and most importantly *finishing* the things he has called us to do—and we do it for his glory, in his strength, to accomplish his goals, then we're wildly successful.

Here's the kicker: being favored includes failing.

If there's one thing we learn from Scripture, it's that God sometimes leads a person to do something, knowing they will fail, and tells them to do it anyway.

In other words, God calls people to fail on purpose, and when they do, they're successful.

You read that correctly.

Sometimes when we pray for God's favor, he responds by *causing* us to fail. He *leads* us to fail. He *puts us* in situations where he *knows* we're going to blow it in epic fashion, and that is all part of his larger plan.

In fact, sometimes one of the clearest signs that we're squarely in the will of God is that when we look back we see a string of abysmal, embarrassing, heart-wrenching failures.

Don't believe me? Just ask Abraham.

The Bible tells us in Genesis 24:1 that "Abraham was now very old, and the LORD had blessed him in every way."

If you're *not* familiar with the story of Abraham, he probably reminds you of the type of person you'd see featured on the cover of *Fortune* magazine, sitting on a hood of his Rolls Royce parked in front of one of his twenty-four homes.

If the Creator of the universe blessed Abraham in *every* way, we Americans assume he'd be the mythical guy everyone holds up as a role model for business and life. He'd have perfect teeth, a beautiful wife, and 2.5 kids who went to Harvard but served the poor on the weekends. To relax, he'd hand out money to the poor while jogging sixteen miles to keep in shape, simultaneously calling various world leaders to try to get them to forgive the debt of African countries so they could afford antiretroviral medications to treat AIDS.

Can you imagine what your life would look like if you could say that God had blessed you not in *some* ways but in *every* way?

The thing is we don't have to imagine.

Abraham was seventy years old when God told him,

> Go from your country, your people and your father's household to the land I will show you.
>
> I will make you a great nation. (Genesis 12:1-2)

Abraham left his father and extended family behind in a city named Haran (in modern-day Turkey) and traveled to the land of Canaan (in modern-day Israel).

When Abraham died at 175 years, I don't see how anyone would have thought his life had been blessed in *most* ways, let alone *every* way. (And yes, he actually lived to 175. See Genesis 25:7. Can you imagine how much his back and knees hurt? Geez!)

The twelfth-century Jewish scholar Maimonides believed there were ten great tests Abraham had to endure.[4]

Test 1. God told Abraham to leave his homeland and sojourn as a stranger into the land of Canaan (Genesis 12:1).

Test 2. As soon as he arrived in the Promised Land he had to face a severe famine, which sent him searching for food in Egypt just to survive (Genesis 12:10).

Test 3. The Egyptians believed Abraham's wife Sarah was so hot that they abducted her and made her one of Pharaoh's concubines, and Abraham told them she was his sister to keep from getting killed (Genesis 12:10-20).

Test 4. Once back in Israel, Abraham was forced to go to war against rival clans just to stay alive and protect his family (Genesis 14:1-24).

Test 5. Abraham and Sarah faced infertility for years. Thus they believed having a child with another woman, Hagar, would allow him to fulfill God's promise to be the progenitor of a great nation (Genesis 16:3).

Test 6. God told Abraham to grab a knife and circumcise himself—Worst. Test. Ever. (Genesis 17:24).

Test 7. As in Egypt, Abraham again feared for his life and passed his wife off as his sister to the king of Gerar, who intended to take her as his wife until God intervened (Genesis 20).

Test 8. Abraham sent his concubine, Hagar, and their child, Ishmael, into the desert to fend for themselves (Genesis 21:9-20).

Test 9. Abraham became estranged from his son Ishmael (Genesis 21:14).

Test 10. God told Abraham to sacrifice his son Isaac on an altar (Genesis 22:2).

To this list of challenges identified by Maimonides, I think there are two more struggles Abraham faced that are worth noting.

~ Abraham lost a beloved family member when he lost his nephew Lot's wife in the destruction of the cities of Sodom and Gomorrah (Genesis 19:26).

~ Since Abraham's wife Sarah died when she was 127 (Genesis 23:1) and Abraham lived until he was 175 (Genesis 25:7), he spent forty-eight years without the love of his life. If you ask me, that was his last and most difficult test of all.

When we look back on the life of Abraham—aside from the moments of happiness that we must discern by reading between the lines—I'm not sure how anyone could describe his life as "blessed in every way."

His life reminds me of a heartbreaking line from the movie *Memoirs of a Geisha*.

The movie tells the story of two young girls sold by their poor parents who cannot afford to keep them any longer. One daughter is sold into prostitution and the other into training to be a geisha. The movie is the story retold through the eyes of the daughter sold into geisha training.

The geisha, now an older woman, narrates the story. She begins, "A story like mine should never be told."

Soon after being sold as a geisha, the girl receives word that her only sister has escaped, never to be seen again, and both of her parents have died. The head mistress mockingly tells the girl, "We are your only family now."

The girl, now an older woman, interjects, "At the temple, there is a poem called *Loss*, carved into the stone. It has three words, but the poet has scratched them out. You cannot read *Loss*, only feel it."[5]

That sense of despair felt by the girl had to be what Abraham felt most of his life. He passed his wife off as his sister, not once but twice. He had a child with another woman, then sent them off to their death in the desert. He faced loneliness in his old age, comparable only to the loss he felt leaving his family in his early years.

Under no definition of the word could anyone look back upon Abraham's life and call him blessed.

Yet God did.

Success is finding favor with God, and that sometimes means we do things that God knows we're going to fail trying.

The failures *are* the blessings.

The lessons learned, the relationships forged, the trust with God that needs to be developed to simply stay alive, let alone persevere—these are all blessings from God.

The good things, the painful things, the boneheaded decisions we make, and the occasional glimpses of spectacular accomplishment in the eyes of the world all park themselves under the same roof called God's divine blessings.

WHY SETTLE FOR SUCCESS WHEN YOU CAN HAVE GOD'S FAVOR?

There's absolutely nothing wrong with wanting to be successful, to be ambitious, and to be 100X used by God (see chap. 1). So long as you are operating under God's definition of success.

So many Christians I meet remind me of Richard, the main character played by Greg Kinnear in the movie *Little Miss Sunshine*. Richard is a struggling motivational speaker who has taken up teaching at the local community college to make ends meet. At the end of a nine-week class titled "Unleash the Winner Inside," Richard concludes his final lecture by saying to the class, "If there's one thing you can take away from the nine weeks we've spent, it should be this: winners and losers. What's the difference?"

His upbeat positivity barely masks his insecurity and frustration as he mouths the words. As he turns the PowerPoint slide, a picture of Darwin's evolution of man appears. On the left is a man hunched over and exasperated. Over his head is written the word "loser." On the right stands a man labeled "winner" with his arms stretched overhead, victorious. He continues,

> Winners see their dreams come true. Winners see what they want; they go out and they get it. They don't hesitate. They don't make excuses. And they don't give up. Losers don't get what they want. They hesitate. They make excuses. And they give up. On themselves and their dreams.

Then he puts his remote down for a final, rousing sendoff. His last words are, "Inside each of you—at the very core of your being—is a Winner waiting to be awakened and unleashed upon the world. I want you to go out into the world and be winners!"[6]

The scene ends with Richard smiling. The camera angle changes so we see him from the back of the room, revealing that there's maybe twenty students filling up a fraction of the available chairs. They clap half-heartedly. Then there's the awkward moment when all you hear is the sound of chairs scraping the floor.

What's so sad about that scene is not just how awkward we feel as we watch the scene play out, but how hollow and inauthentic it can come across to want to be successful for the sake of success, which everyone can see, except Richard himself.

Winners don't carry crosses.

Winners don't serve.

Winners don't give away money.

Winners don't let people walk all over them and choose not to retaliate.

Winners don't have time to care for people who have chosen to be losers (e.g., the poor, the hurting, the depressed, the confused, the average).

Here's the sad thing: *I'm* Richard. I'm that guy.

I want to be successful. I want to win at everything I do.

The great Chinese Christian author Watchman Nee wrote, "I appreciate the blessed fact of God's forgiveness, but I want something more than that: *I want deliverance. I need forgiveness for what I have done, but I need also deliverance from what I am.*"[7]

I know God has saved me from the punishment of my sins in hell. What I really need is salvation from the punishment of my sins on earth. I need to change, but so often I can't.

I'm saddened by the persistent sins, personality flaws, relational patterns, and destructive behaviors that I can't shake and that always end up hurting those I care about the most. These deep, ancient fissures in my character cause more distress with each passing year.

None of my ongoing struggles and flaws trouble me more than my need to be successful. I don't *want* to be successful. I *need* to be successful. There's a troubling difference between the two.

I have been enslaved by the American definition of success, which psychologist Richard Beck so beautifully elucidates in *The Slavery of Death*:

Every American is thus ingrained with the duty to look well, to seem fine, to exclude from the fabric of his or her normal life any evidence of decay and death and helplessness. The ethic I have outlined here is often called the ethic of success. I prefer to call it the ethic of avoidance.... Persons are considered a success not because they attain some remarkable goal, but because their lives do not betray marks of failure or depression, helplessness or sickness. When they are asked how they are, they really can say and really do say, "Fine ... fine."[8]

I dread insignificance. I dread being average. Deep down inside I know this is wrong. I know my significance is found in Christ. I know my identity is to be found solely in what Christ did for me on the cross. I know that being loved by God should be enough.

But if I'm being perfectly honest, most days it's not. That's just reality. Which is why I've been learning, like the prophet Samuel in the Old Testament, to "grow in ... favor with the LORD" (1 Samuel 2:26).

One does not change overnight.

Unfortunately.

CONCLUSION

THE OTHER DAY I WAS DRIVING ON a freeway in our area, one that backs up for over an hour going in and out of downtown Philadelphia at rush hour.

I made the mistake of jumping onto it because I was in a hurry to get somewhere (in the middle of the day, so I thought I was safe) when out of nowhere I pulled up on a car that was driving a leisurely 52 mph in the left-hand passing lane.

The Bible tells us that there's a special place in hell reserved for murderers, terrorists, and people who drive 52 mph in the left-hand lane on a crowded freeway.

As I pulled up on this car I flashed my high beams a few times.

Nothing.

He didn't have the courtesy to move to the right.

Flashed my lights again.

Nothing. He ignored me.

I tried my "lean forward with a penetrating glance and squinted eyes" look to see if he'd get the hint of what I was trying to say to him in his rearview mirror.

To my surprise, again, no reaction.

Pressed for time, I whipped my car over to the right-hand lane, sped up, and floored it to get in front of him.

The late standup comedian George Carlin used to say that anybody driving slower than you is an idiot, and anyone going faster than you is a maniac, so as I passed him I made sure to frown, shrug my shoulders, lift my right hand into the air, and mouth the words "Hey moron!" as I sped by.

This turned out to be kinda awkward because he was a member of my church.

As luck would have it, the reason this inconsiderate, highly rude and uncaring church member was completely ruining my day by going slow in the left-hand lane was there an accident ahead. Either he knew about the fender bender ahead from listening to KYW 1060 AM (the traffic station everyone in the Philadelphia metro area listens to in the morning), or he was simply paying attention to what was ahead, something I obviously was not doing.

Either way, I was rather embarrassed.

Sort of like how I feel when I go back and think about times I've yelled at God for allowing painful things to happen in my life.

I have three friends right now whose sons are doing drugs. I have more friends than I can count who are fighting cancer. If I told you how many couples in my church have great marriages on the outside but are a wreck on the inside, you wouldn't believe me.

I know great Christian people who can't find work, don't know where they're going to be a year from now, can't stop drinking, and can't imagine what they're going to do in the wake of their spouses cheating on them. It pains me to type this, but I know a Christian couple who would be amazing parents if they could only have a baby.

How else am I to respond when I pray to an all-powerful deity who has the power to fix these problems, but chooses not to?

The great nineteenth-century spiritual writer George Mac-Donald observed, "Man finds it hard to get what he wants, because he does not want the best; God finds it hard to give, because He would give the best, and man will not take it."[1]

Looking back at where we've been and what we've discovered together about God's favor, I can see this about myself.

There are aspects of God's favor that anyone would surely want—his provision, intervention, and confirmation of his will—but the other things, who in their right mind would want those?

Who would want to fail on purpose, get sick on purpose, or be forced into obscurity? On the surface, let's admit we'd be weird to actually want those things.

Unless, of course, our eyes are looking farther down the road. Unless we're looking at the bigger picture. Unless we're thinking about how God can use our pain to affect people generations from now, just not this very minute.

How can we discipline ourselves to keep our eyes down the road? What can we do that will help us want *whichever* type of favor God chooses to bestow, not just the "good stuff" the televangelists train us to keep asking for and expecting?

In *My Utmost for His Highest*, Oswald Chambers staunchly confessed, "He can crumple me up or exalt me; He can do anything He chooses."[2]

How can we train ourselves to think like that? That's Mother Teresa or apostle Paul type of faith.

3,743 days. That's about how long it takes, I believe, to start thinking like Oswald Chambers.

It's also, ironically, the exact number of days I estimated that our family prayed together at the dinner table when I was growing up.

Calculating that number was surprisingly easy.

I took out Friday nights because growing up, that was pizza night. Everyone was responsible for praying their own prayer on the way to sacking Dad as he walked through the door with the warm Massey's Pizza box under his arm.

Then I removed Saturdays and Sundays from the tally. Weekends were survival of the fittest. We ate between games, trips to the grandparents, and so on. We prayed for sure, but it wasn't routine. So no prayers counted for those days.

That left Monday through Thursday nights. On those days we prayed before dinner every single night, without fail. Except for the time when I was fourteen and tried to back the car down the driveway to shoot basketball and accidentally ran over the mailbox. We didn't pray that night. But that was it.

Usually, Dad prayed, but we'd all take turns.

That means we prayed

4 days a week

x 52 weeks a year

x 18 years

= 3,744 days

− the day I killed the mailbox

= 3,743 total times we prayed as a family before dinner

Some Christians don't place a high value on praying before a meal. That's a mistake. I believe that saying grace before dinner ranks second only behind going to church as the most important thing parents can do to impact their children spiritually.

There are five things that happen when we pray together as a family before meals.

1. Praying before meals marks our meal together as a sacred pause in our family's day. Flip through the Gospels, and it becomes apparent rather quickly that sharing a meal entailed more than the consumption of food. Stories were shared. The day was recounted. Prayer simply invites God to be a part of the conversation that follows.

2. Praying before meals gives parents the chance to model that God is important. In his book *Blue Like Jazz*, Donald Miller observes, "Sometimes you have to watch somebody love something before you can love it yourself."[3] I agree. For 3,743 days I had the privilege of watching my parents close their eyes, bow their heads, and say, "Let's be thankful."

3. Praying before meals prompts lively discussions about God and the Bible. After praying, I remember my sisters and I asking questions like, How do you know God can even hear us? How do we know there is a God? If God answers prayer, what about the people who _____ [insert tragic accident that happened that day]? No question was out of bounds.

4. Praying before meals opens the door to resolving conflict. If I did something that day that made my sisters want to punch me in the face (usually for good reason), being forced to bow our heads and pray almost always ended with us raising our heads and going after each other, like seconds later. In the same way the body naturally moves to expunge a splinter, taking a moment to focus on God seemed to take us right to what was on each other's minds.

5. *Praying before meals teaches kids to pray even when they don't feel like it.* Growing up, whenever I was mad, preoccupied, or in a hurry, the last thing I wanted to do was pray before meals. But my parents made sure we did anyway. The funny thing is my reasons for not wanting to pray when I was a kid are no different than the reasons I don't want to pray today. Praying at each meal taught me to discipline myself and pray in spite of my feelings, not because of them.

"Sometimes you have to watch somebody love something before you can love it yourself."

I believe that.

One does not magically appear fully devout as a Christ-follower like Oswald Chambers, straight out of the womb. We don't naturally trust what we can't see. We don't naturally understand how to pray to Someone who doesn't talk back. We don't intuitively lift our eyes to see beyond our own difficulty and pain.

This is especially true when it comes to believing and accepting *all* the ways God favors us, not just the ones we like.

Faith is something that's modeled, not taught.

My parents knew, like all wise spiritual mentors, that *until* you believe something in your heart, you keep confessing it with your mouth as you watch someone else who believes it in *their* heart.

You keep praying when you don't feel like it, because that's what *they* do.

You keep trusting when you're angry, because you see *them* react that way.

You keep believing when you can't see that far down the road, because you've learned to trust the God *they've* learned to trust.

Psalm 84:11 says,

For the LORD God is a sun and shield;
   the LORD bestows favor and honor;
no good thing does he withhold
   from those whose walk is blameless.

I believe this verse because I stand on the shoulders of great men and women of faith—starting with my parents—who through thousands of years of suffering have come to believe that this verse is true.

There will be times when we'll be crumpled.

There will be times when we'll be exalted.

But no good thing will he withhold from us.

Ever.

NOTES

INTRODUCTION

[1]John Climacus, *The Ladder of Divine Ascent* (Mahwah, NJ: Paulist Press, 1982), 217.

[2]Augustine, *Confessions*, trans. Henry Chadwick (New York: Oxford University Press, 1998), 40.

1 GOD'S FAVOR

[1]Elton Trueblood, *Alternative to Futility* (New York: Harper, 1948), 75.

[2]Bob Buford, *Half Time: Moving from Success to Significance* (Grand Rapids: Zondervan, 1994), 24.

[3]Oswald Chambers, *My Utmost for His Highest* (Grand Rapids: Discovery House, 1992), March 24 entry.

[4]Augustine, *The Confessions of St. Augustine* (New York: P. F. Collier, 1909), 47.

2 INVOLUNTARY PERSEVERANCE

[1]Some of the material in this and the preceding paragraphs were first published in Brian Jones, "Why Senior Pastors Must Be Both Scholarly and Pragmatic," Pastors.com, January 4, 2011, http://pastors.com/why-senior -pastors-must-be-both-scholarly-and-pragmatic; and was reposted in *Ministry Today*, January 11, 2016, https://ministrytodaymag.com/leadership /higher-education/22504-why-senior-pastors-must-be-both-scholarly-and -pragmatic.

[2]François Fénelon, *Let Go* (New Kensington, PA: Whitaker House, 1973), 4.

[3]David Whyte, *Crossing the Unknown Sea* (New York City: Riverhead Books, 2001), 132.

[4]A. W. Tozer, *The Pursuit of Man* (Camp Hill: Christian Publications, 1950), 45-46.

[5]Oswald Chambers, *My Utmost for His Highest* (Grand Rapids: Discovery House, 1992), January 13.

3 HOLY DISCONTENT

[1]Homer, *The Odyssey*, trans. Robert Fagles (New York: Penguin Group, 1996), 214.

[2]Ibid.

[3]Kathleen Norris, *Acedia & Me* (New York: Riverhead Books, 2008), 3.

[4]Mervin Breneman, *Ezra, Nehemiah, Esther*, New American Commentary (Nashville: B&H, 1993), 42.

[5]Elizabeth Barrett Browning, *Aurora Leigh* (London: Chapman & Hall, 1857), 39.

[6]Meister Eckhart, *Meister Eckhart*, Classics of Western Spirituality (Mahwah, NJ: Paulist Press, 1981), 262.

[7]Suzanne Collins, *Catching Fire*, The Hunger Games (New York: Scholastic Press, 2009), 31-32.

[8]Søren Kierkegaard, *Sickness unto Death* (New York: Start Publishing, 2012), 5.

[9]Evagrius of Pontus, "On Prayer," in *The Orthodox Way* (New York: St. Vladimir's Seminary Press, 1979), 128-29.

[10]Jürgen Moltmann, *Jürgen Moltmann Collected Readings*, ed. Margaret Kohl (Minneapolis: Fortress Press, 2014), 13.

4 INTENTIONAL OBSCURITY

[1]Vincent van Gogh, *The Letters of Vincent van Gogh* (New York: Penguin Classics, 1998), 57.

[2]Ibid., 58.

[3]Ibid., 55.

[4]Vincent van Gogh, letter to Theo van Gogh, November 3, 1881, www.vangoghletters.org/vg/letters/let179/letter.html#translation.

[5]Vincent van Gogh, *Van Gogh* (Hastings, UK: Delphi Classics, 2014), 2855.

[6]Vincent van Gogh, *Dear Theo: The Autobiography of Vincent van Gogh*, ed. Irving Stone (New York City: Penguin Books, 1937), 47.

[7]Van Gogh, *Letters of Vincent van* Gogh, 54.

[8]"Obscurity," *The American Heritage Dictionary of the English Language*, 5th ed. (Boston: Houghton Mifflin, 2016), 1216.

[9]Oswald Chambers, *My Utmost for His Highest* (New York: Dodd, Mead, 1935), 188.

[10]Brené Brown, *Daring Greatly* (New York: Penguin Group, 2012), Kindle ed.

[11]Frederick Buechner, *Wishful Thinking: A Theological ABC* (New York: Harper & Row, 1973), 95.

[12]Philip Yancey, *Finding God in Unexpected Places* (New York: Random House, 2005), 212.

[13]Catherine Marshall, *A Man Called Peter: The Story of Peter Marshall* (Grand Rapids: Chosen Books, 1951), 86.

5 SUPERNATURAL PROVISION

[1]D. A. Carson, *Matthew*, Expositor's Bible Commentary 1 (Grand Rapids: Zondervan, 1995), 187.

[2]Hillel popularized seven strategies for biblical interpretations and argumentation, which are often called the "Seven Middoth" of Hillel—or the seven rules.

[3]A. W. Tozer, *Knowledge of the Holy* (San Francisco: HarperOne, 1978), 1.

[4]Clement of Alexandria, *Complete Works of Clement of Alexandria* (Hastings, UK: Delphi Classics, 2016), 180.

6 BODILY AFFLICTION

[1]Søren Kierkegaard, *Ethics, Love, and Faith in Kierkegaard* (Bloomington: Indiana University Press, 2008), 123.

[2]Oswald Chambers, *My Utmost for His Highest* (New York: Dodd, Mead, 1935), 13.

[3]Dietrich Bonhoeffer, *A Testament to Freedom: The Essential Writings of Dietrich Bonhoeffer*, ed. Geffrey B. Kelly and F. Burton Nelson (New York: Harper One, 1995), 445.

[4]Thomas à Kempis, *The Imitation of Christ* (Dublin: James Duffy, Wellington Quay, 1850), 296.

7 INTERPERSONAL INTERVENTION

[1]Oswald Chambers, *The Highest Good* (Grand Rapids: Discovery House, 1965), 30.

[2]William Harley, *Love Busters* (Grand Rapids: Revell, 1992), 5.

8 REDEMPTIVE POVERTY

[1]Brian Jones, *Getting Rid of the Gorilla* (Cincinnati: Standard Publishing, 2008), 198.

[2]Jean Delumeau, *History of Paradise: The Garden of Eden in Myth and Tradition* (Champaign: University of Illinois Press, 2000), 40.

[3]Flavius Josephus, *Josephus: The Complete Works*, Christian Classics Ethereal Library, accessed January 5, 2017, www.ccel.org/ccel/josephus/complete.i.html.

[4]Joshua Becker, "21 Surprising Statistics That Reveal How Much Stuff We Actually Own," *Becoming Minimalist* (blog), accessed September 13, 2017, www.becomingminimalist.com/clutter-stats.

[5]Seneca, *Seneca's Letters from a Stoic* (Mineola, NY: Dover Publications, 2016), 40.

10 STRATEGIC FAILURE

[1]Henry Blackaby and Richard Blackaby, *Spiritual Leadership* (Nashville: B&H, 2001), 202.

[2]Warren Bennis and Patricia Ward Biederman, *Organizing Genius* (New York: Basic Books, 1997), 208.

[3]Barbara Brown Taylor, "Divine Subtraction," *Christian Century*, November 3, 1999, www.christiancentury.org/article/2011-07/divine-subtraction.

[4]Moses Maimonides, *The Guide for the Perplexed*, trans. M. Friedlander (New York: E. P. Dutton, 1919), 304.

[5]Robin Swicord, *Memoirs of a Geisha*, directed by Rob Marshall (Los Angeles: Columbia Pictures, 2005).

[6]Michael Arndt, *Little Miss Sunshine*, directed by Jonathan Dayton and Valerie Faris (Los Angeles: Fox Searchlight Pictures, 2006).

[7]Watchman Nee, *The Finest of the Wheat* (New York: Christian Fellowship Publishers, 1993), 554; emphasis added.

[8]Richard Beck, *The Slavery of Death* (Eugene, OR: Cascade Books, 2014), 34.

CONCLUSION

[1]George MacDonald, *Unspoken Sermons* (New York: Cosimo, 1867), 207.

[2]Oswald Chambers, *My Utmost for His Highest* (Grand Rapids: Discovery House, 1992), November 10.

[3]Donald Miller, *Blue Like Jazz* (Nashville: Thomas Nelson, 2003), vii.